INNER REFLECTIONS

ENGAGEMENT CALENDAR 2027

SELECTIONS FROM THE WRITINGS OF
PARAMAHANSA YOGANANDA

SELF-REALIZATION FELLOWSHIP

Front Cover:
Lake Minamiinaga, Yamanashi, Japan
Photograph by Daniel Kordan
Design by Shawn Freeman

Note: *Holidays and other observed dates are included for the United States (U.S.), Canada, United Kingdom (U.K.), Australia, and New Zealand (N.Z.).*
Moon phases, equinoxes, and solstices are based on Pacific Standard Time (UTC – 8 hours).

Printed using vegetable-based, petroleum-free inks on FSC (Forest Stewardship Council) certified papers.

Printed in Italy
4884-J8932

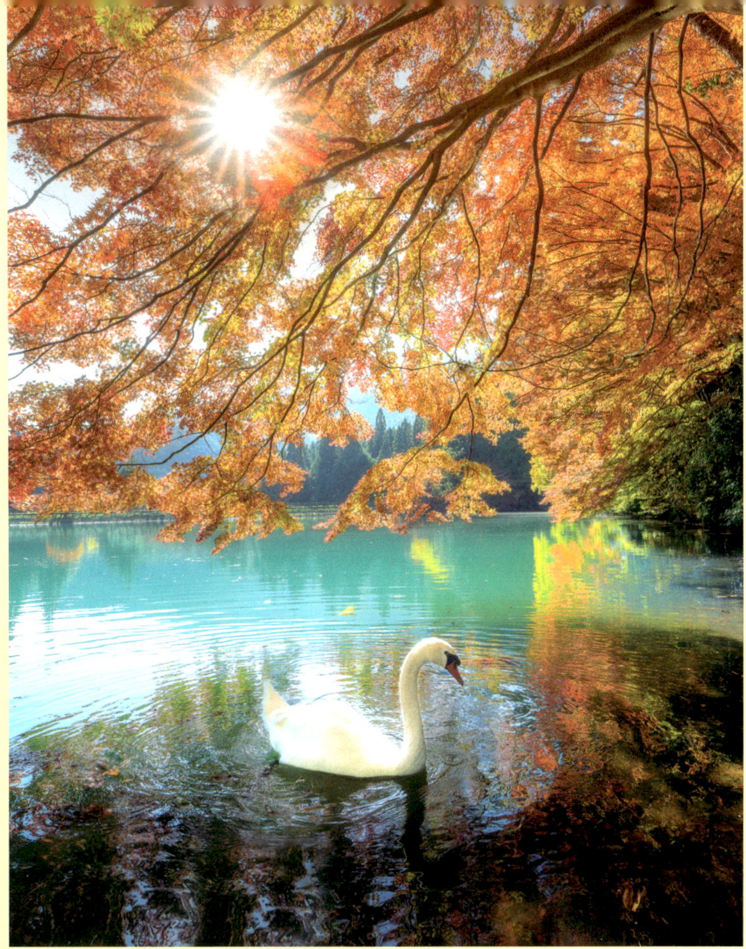

Beholding the blossoms of the earth and the starry flowers in the infinite fields of the sky, how can one not wonder, "Is there a hidden Beauty behind these finite patterns?"... The blossoms of life in the garden of earthly existence are enchanting to behold. But somewhere there is a fount of Beauty and Intelligence, even more enthralling, from which we have come and into which we shall merge again.

—Paramahansa Yogananda

THE PHOTOGRAPHS IN THIS CALENDAR are accompanied by selections from the writings of Paramahansa Yogananda, whose timeless and universal teachings have awakened many — of all races, cultures, and creeds — to a deeper awareness of the one reality that sustains and unites us all.

Whether spread over the vast heavens or hidden in the exquisite delicacy of a tiny flower, nature's beauty is always beckoning, inviting us to look behind the outward form and sense the presence of God within.

We hope that the thoughts and images in these pages will bring you inspiration and encouragement in the days and weeks of the coming year.

Lake Minamiinaga, Yamanashi, Japan Photograph by Daniel Kordan

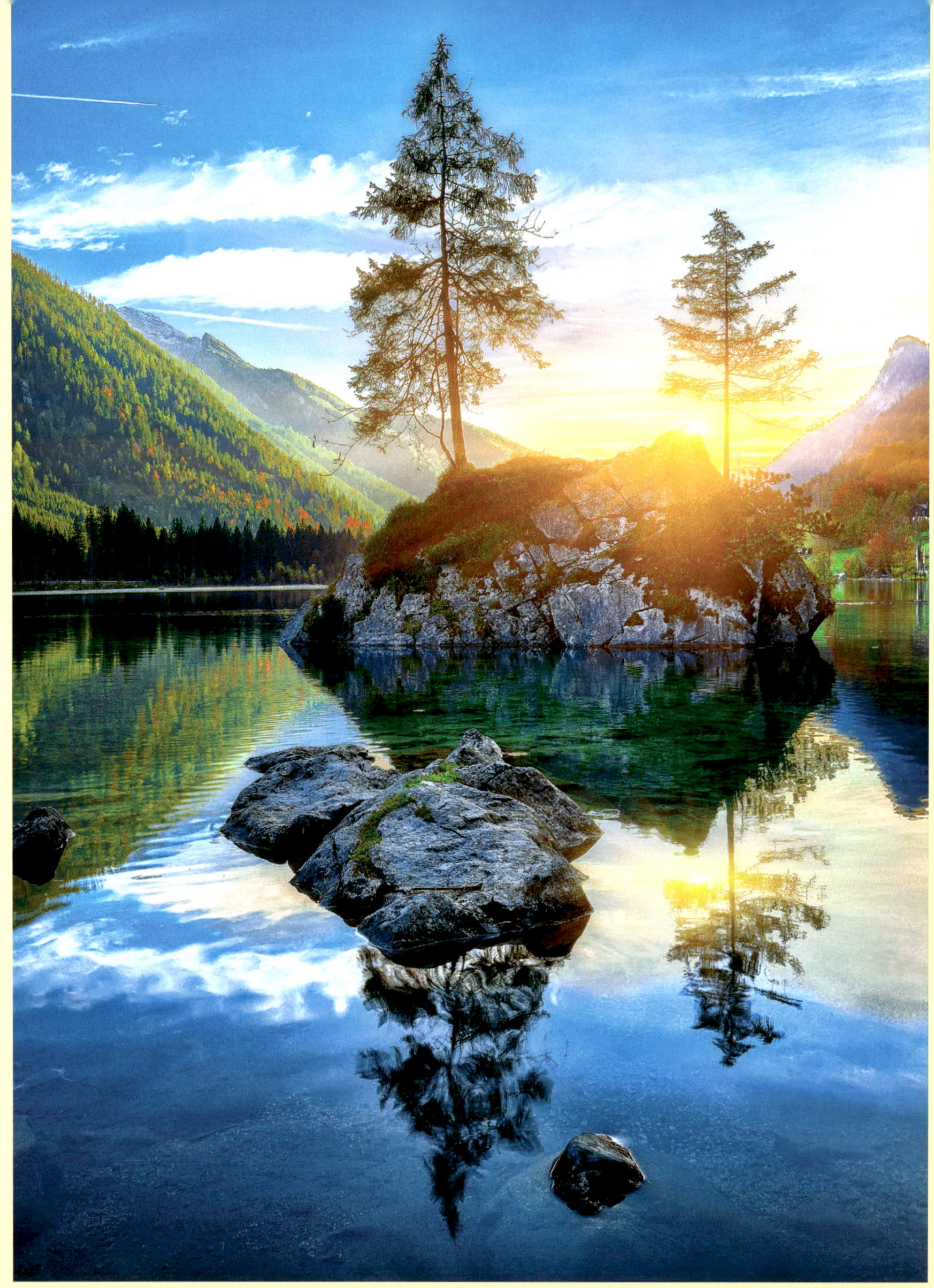

Enter the portals of the New Year with new hope.
Remember you are a child of God.
It lies with you as to what you are going to be.

—Paramahansa Yogananda

Hintersee Lake, near Ramsau, Germany   Photograph by Vadym Lavra

December/January

28
monday

29
tuesday

30
wednesday

Last Quarter ◐

31
thursday

1
friday

New Year's Day

2
saturday

3
sunday

December 2026

S	M	T	W	T	F	S
		1	2	3	4	5
6	7	8	9	10	11	12
13	14	15	16	17	18	19
20	21	22	23	24	25	26
27	28	29	30	31		

January

S	M	T	W	T	F	S
					1	2
3	4	5	6	7	8	9
10	11	12	13	14	15	16
17	18	19	20	21	22	23
24/31	25	26	27	28	29	30

January

4
monday

5
tuesday
Paramahansa Yogananda's Birthday

6
wednesday

7
thursday
New Moon ●

8
friday

9
saturday

10
sunday

JANUARY						
S	M	T	W	T	F	S
					1	2
3	4	5	6	7	8	9
10	11	12	13	14	15	16
17	18	19	20	21	22	23
24/31	25	26	27	28	29	30

FEBRUARY						
S	M	T	W	T	F	S
	1	2	3	4	5	6
7	8	9	10	11	12	13
14	15	16	17	18	19	20
21	22	23	24	25	26	27
28						

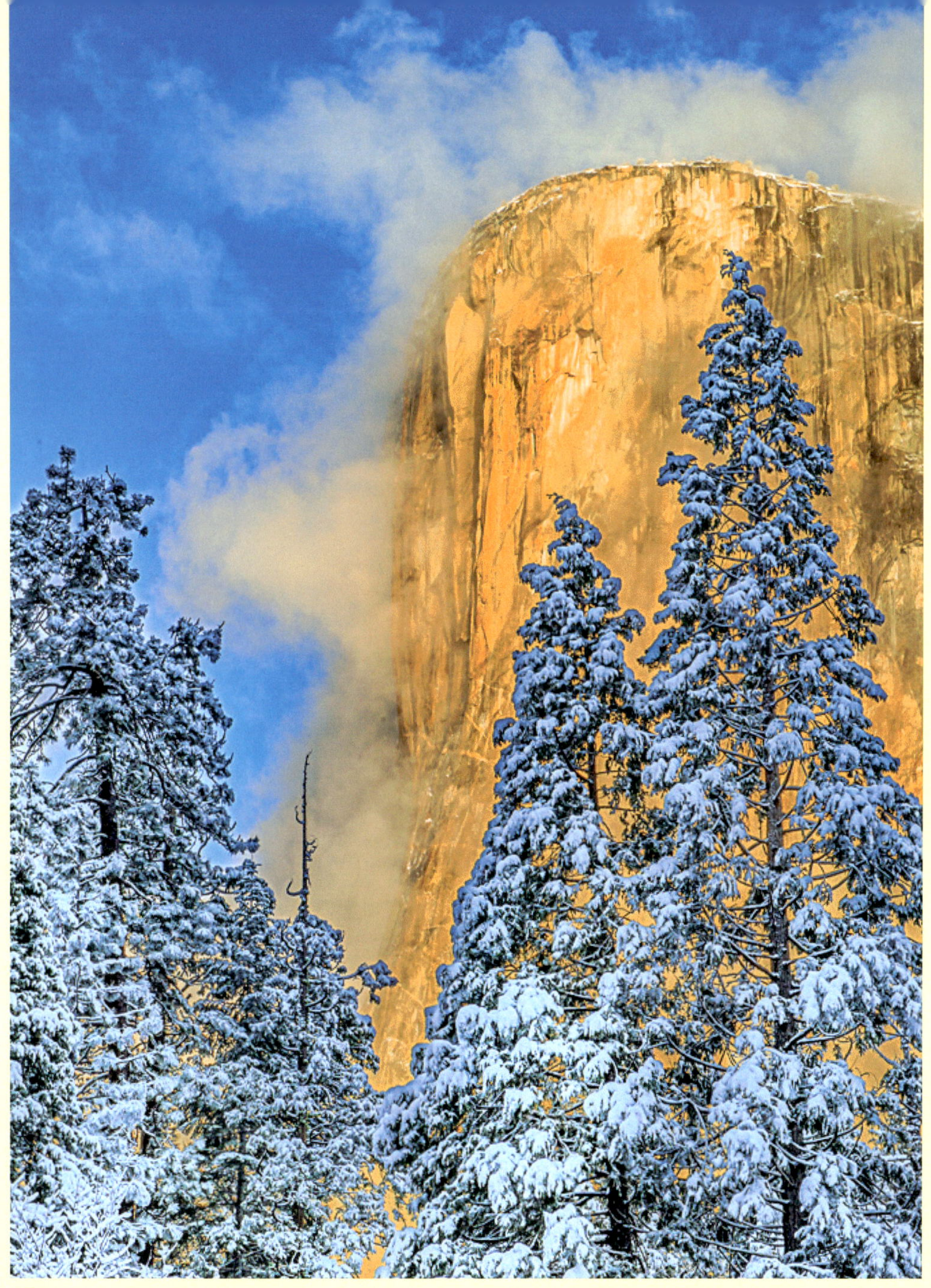

On that day when your soul shall remember its divine origin,
your consciousness will live again in the great mansion of Spirit.

—Paramahansa Yogananda

El Capitan, Yosemite National Park, California   Photograph by Jeff Foott

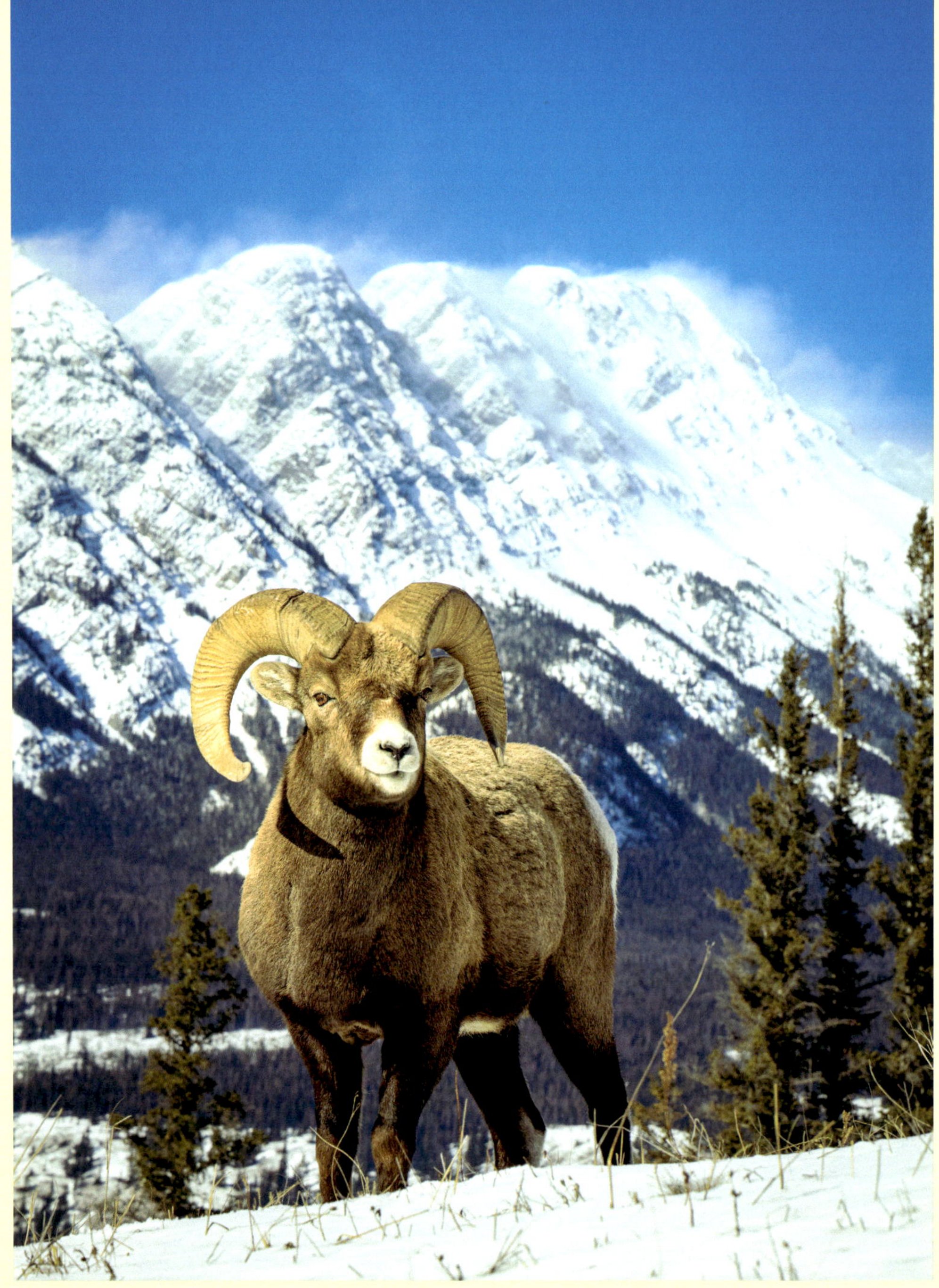

Whenever situations demand discrimination and wise action, recall immediately the calmness experienced during and after meditation: enter into this mood, and meet every challenge from this calm center.

—Paramahansa Yogananda

Bighorn Sheep, Jasper National Park, Alberta, Canada   Photograph by Donald M. Jones/Minden Pictures

January

11
monday

12
tuesday

13
wednesday

14
thursday

First Quarter ◐

15
friday

16
saturday

17
sunday

January

S	M	T	W	T	F	S
					1	2
3	4	5	6	7	8	9
10	11	12	13	14	15	16
17	18	19	20	21	22	23
24/31	25	26	27	28	29	30

February

S	M	T	W	T	F	S
	1	2	3	4	5	6
7	8	9	10	11	12	13
14	15	16	17	18	19	20
21	22	23	24	25	26	27
28						

January

18
monday

Martin Luther King, Jr.'s Birthday (Observed)

19
tuesday

20
wednesday

21
thursday

22
friday

Full Moon ◯

23
saturday

24
sunday

JANUARY

S	M	T	W	T	F	S
					1	2
3	4	5	6	7	8	9
10	11	12	13	14	15	16
17	18	19	20	21	22	23
24/31	25	26	27	28	29	30

FEBRUARY

S	M	T	W	T	F	S
	1	2	3	4	5	6
7	8	9	10	11	12	13
14	15	16	17	18	19	20
21	22	23	24	25	26	27
28						

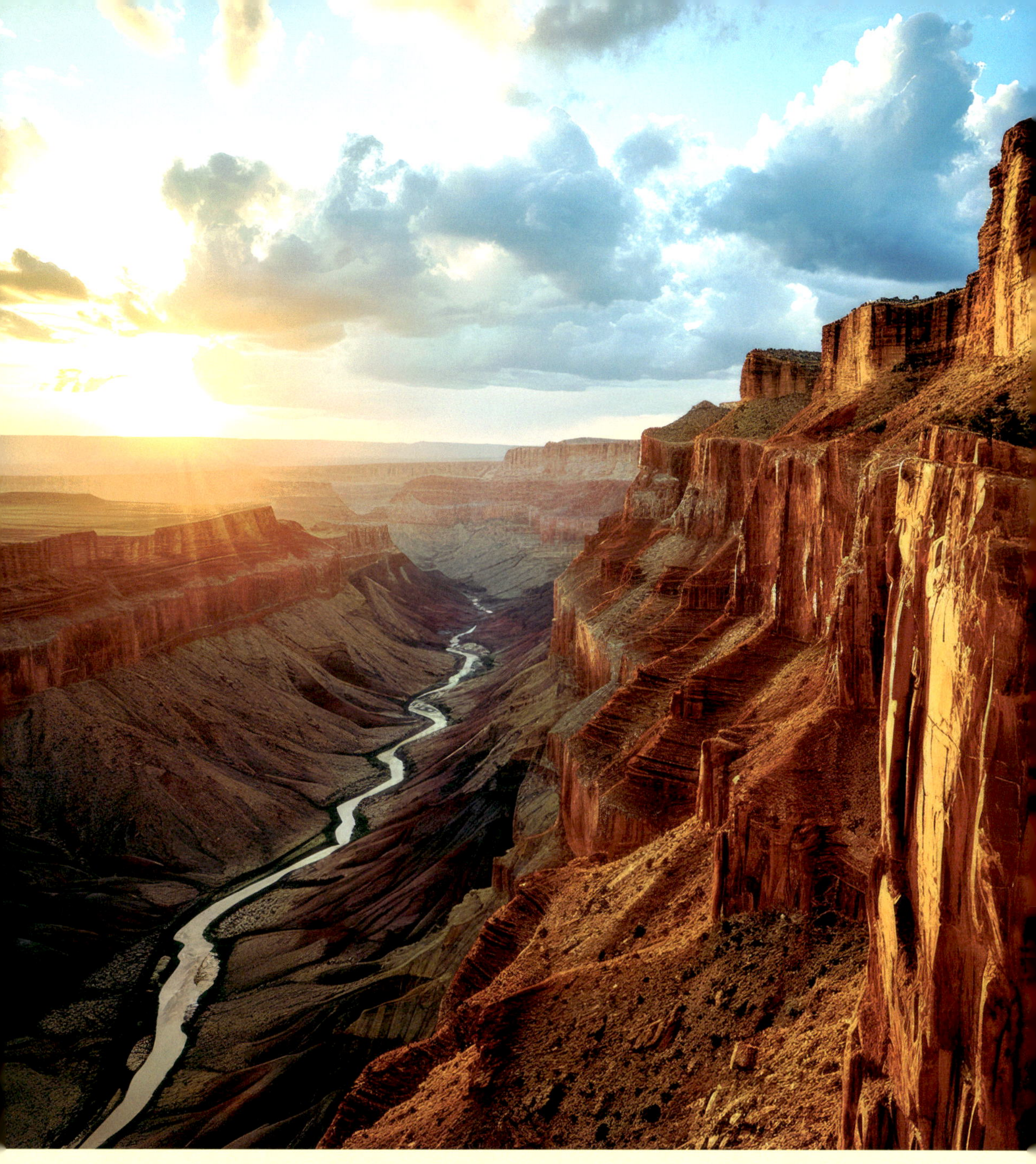

You must be calm to be successful....Through the portals of silence the healing sun of wisdom and peace will shine upon you.

—Paramahansa Yogananda

Grand Canyon National Park, Arizona   Photograph by Vadym Loginov/Superstock

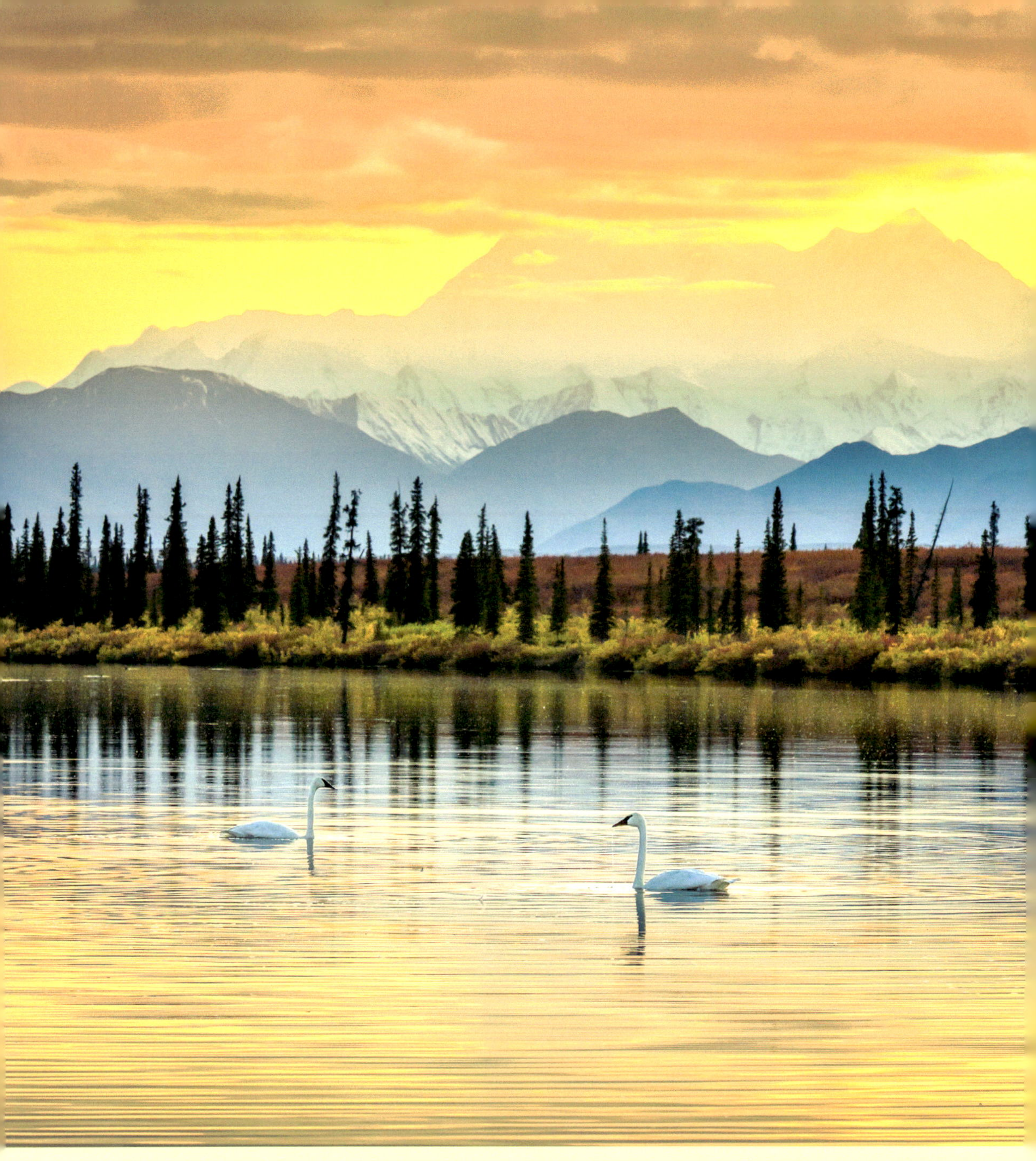

If at this moment you could completely calm your body, your thoughts, and your emotions, you would instantly become aware of your true Self, the soul, and of your great body of the universe.

—Paramahansa Yogananda

Denali National Park, Alaska   Photograph by Patrick Endres

January

25
monday

Australia Day (Australia)

26
tuesday

27
wednesday

28
thursday

Last Quarter ◑

29
friday

JANUARY

S	M	T	W	T	F	S
					1	2
3	4	5	6	7	8	9
10	11	12	13	14	15	16
17	18	19	20	21	22	23
24/31	25	26	27	28	29	30

30
saturday

FEBRUARY

S	M	T	W	T	F	S
	1	2	3	4	5	6
7	8	9	10	11	12	13
14	15	16	17	18	19	20
21	22	23	24	25	26	27
28						

31
sunday

February

1
monday

2
tuesday

3
wednesday

4
thursday

5
friday

6
saturday

New Moon ●

7
sunday

FEBRUARY

S	M	T	W	T	F	S
	1	2	3	4	5	6
7	8	9	10	11	12	13
14	15	16	17	18	19	20
21	22	23	24	25	26	27
28						

MARCH

S	M	T	W	T	F	S
	1	2	3	4	5	6
7	8	9	10	11	12	13
14	15	16	17	18	19	20
21	22	23	24	25	26	27
28	29	30	31			

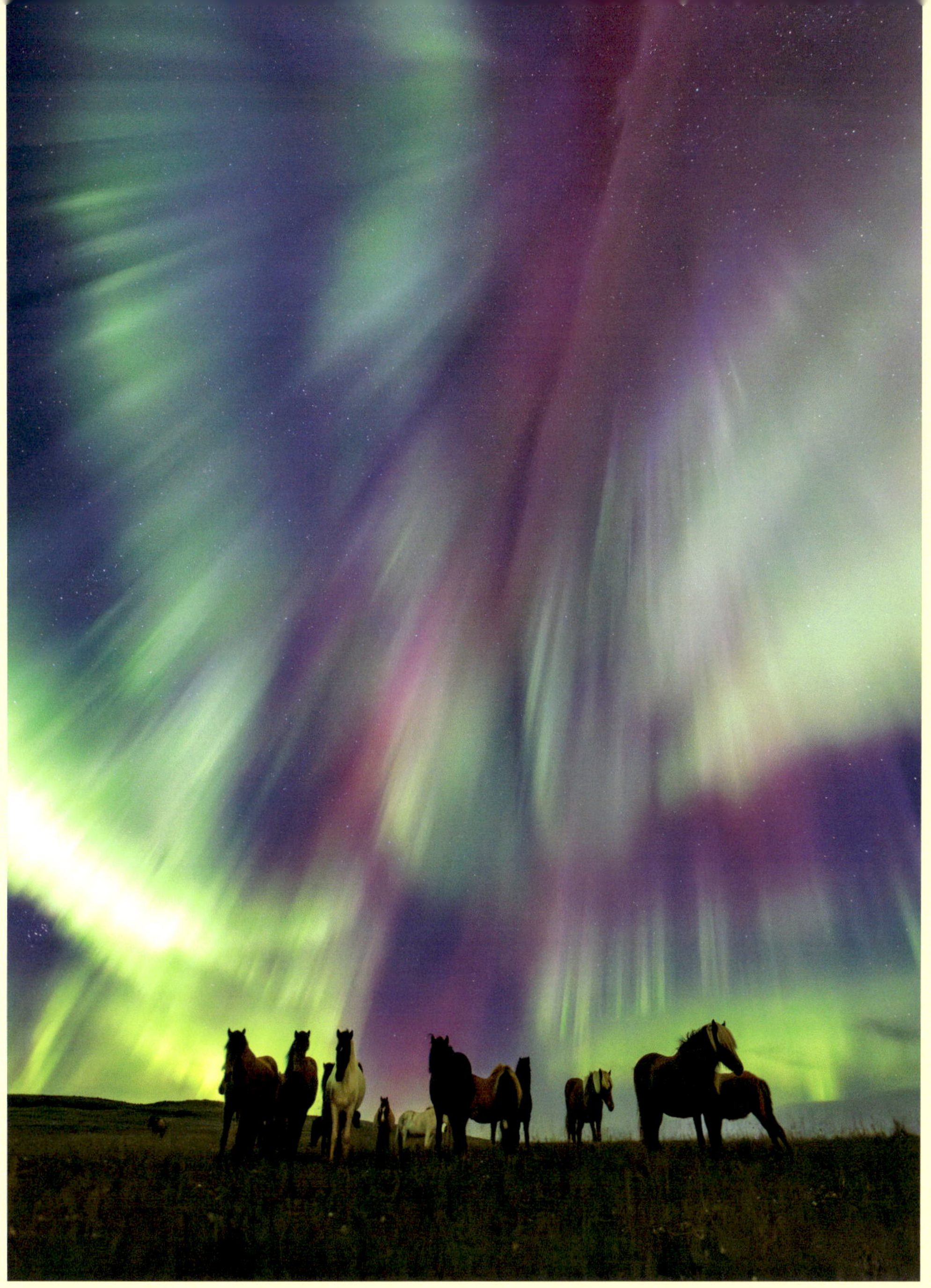

When you try to experience your spiritual convictions,
another world begins to open up to you.

—Paramahansa Yogananda

Icelandic Horses and aurora borealis   Photograph by Espen Bergersen/Minden Pictures

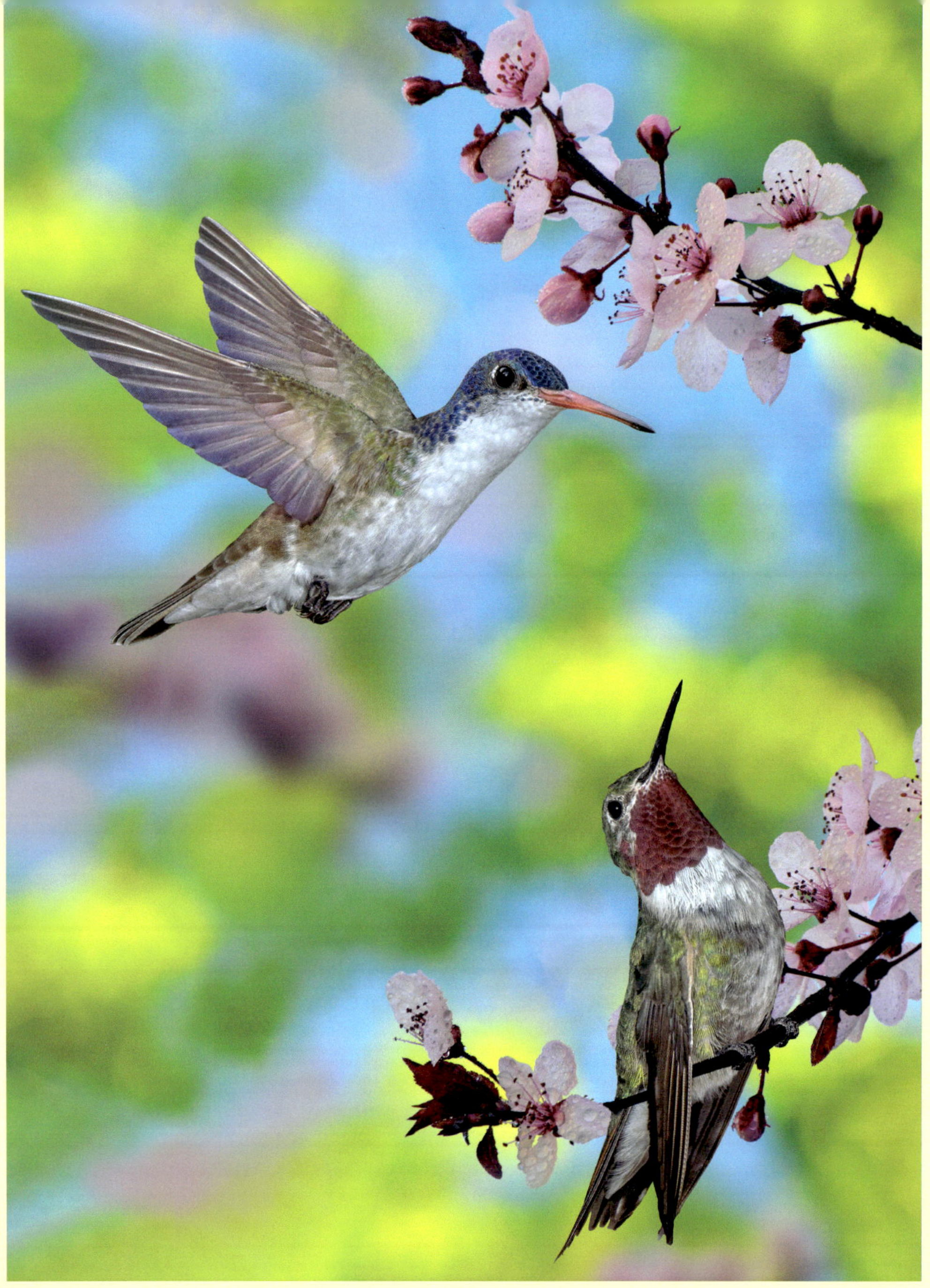

Love cannot be had for the asking; it comes only as a gift from the heart of another.

—Paramahansa Yogananda

Violet-crowned and Broad-tailed Hummingbirds, Sierra Vista, Arizona Photograph by Dean Hueber

February

8
monday

9
tuesday

10
wednesday

11
thursday

12
friday

First Quarter ◐

13
saturday

St. Valentine's Day

14
sunday

FEBRUARY

S	M	T	W	T	F	S
	1	2	3	4	5	6
7	8	9	10	11	12	13
14	15	16	17	18	19	20
21	22	23	24	25	26	27
28						

MARCH

S	M	T	W	T	F	S
	1	2	3	4	5	6
7	8	9	10	11	12	13
14	15	16	17	18	19	20
21	22	23	24	25	26	27
28	29	30	31			

February

15
monday

Presidents' Day

16
tuesday

17
wednesday

18
thursday

19
friday

20
saturday

Full Moon ○

21
sunday

FEBRUARY

S	M	T	W	T	F	S
	1	2	3	4	5	6
7	8	9	10	11	12	13
14	15	16	17	18	19	20
21	22	23	24	25	26	27
28						

MARCH

S	M	T	W	T	F	S
	1	2	3	4	5	6
7	8	9	10	11	12	13
14	15	16	17	18	19	20
21	22	23	24	25	26	27
28	29	30	31			

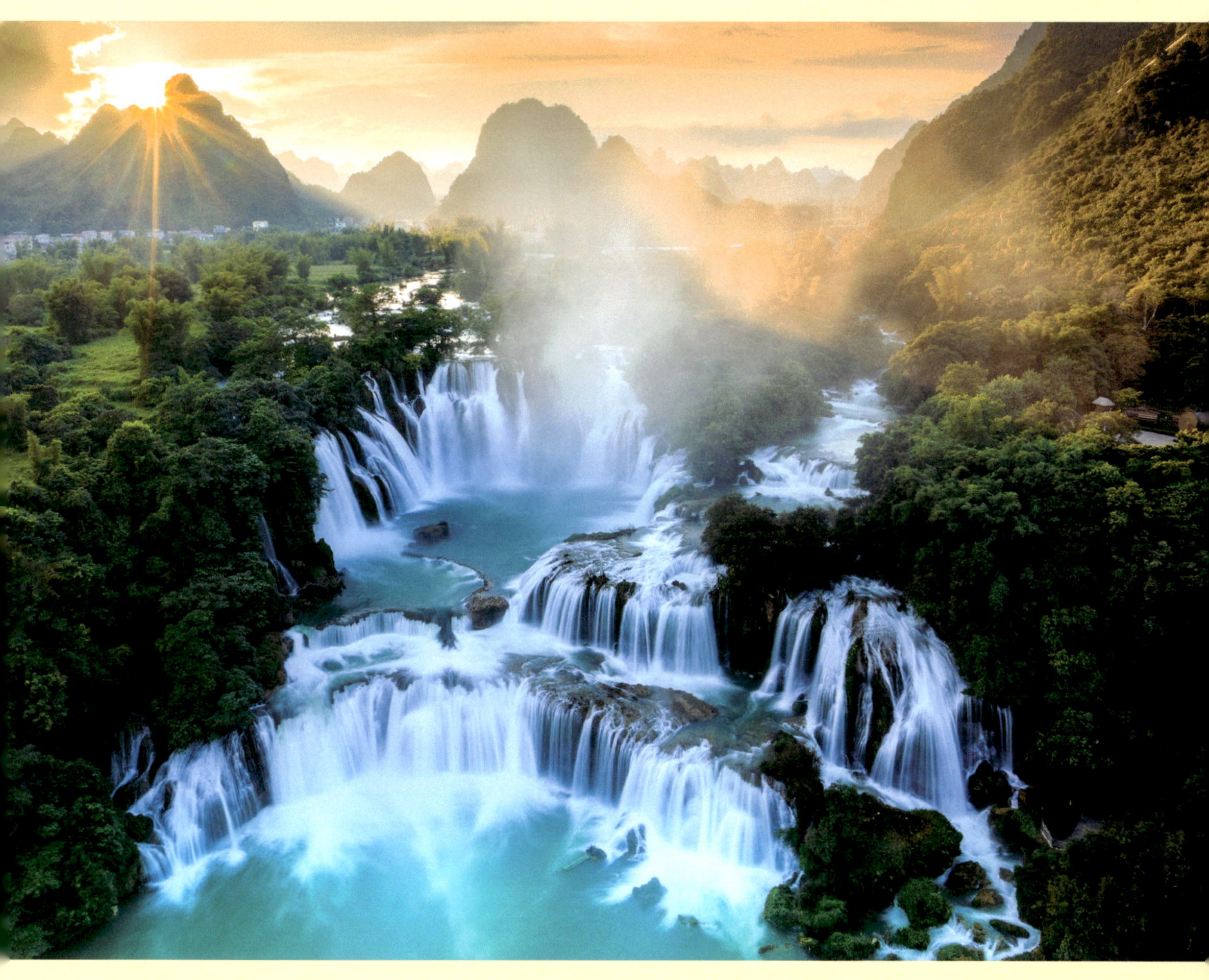

*If you are conscious of the Source of this life,
you will know how to draw continuously on its sustaining power.*

—Paramahansa Yogananda

Bản Giốc Falls, Vietnam Photograph by Daniel Kordan

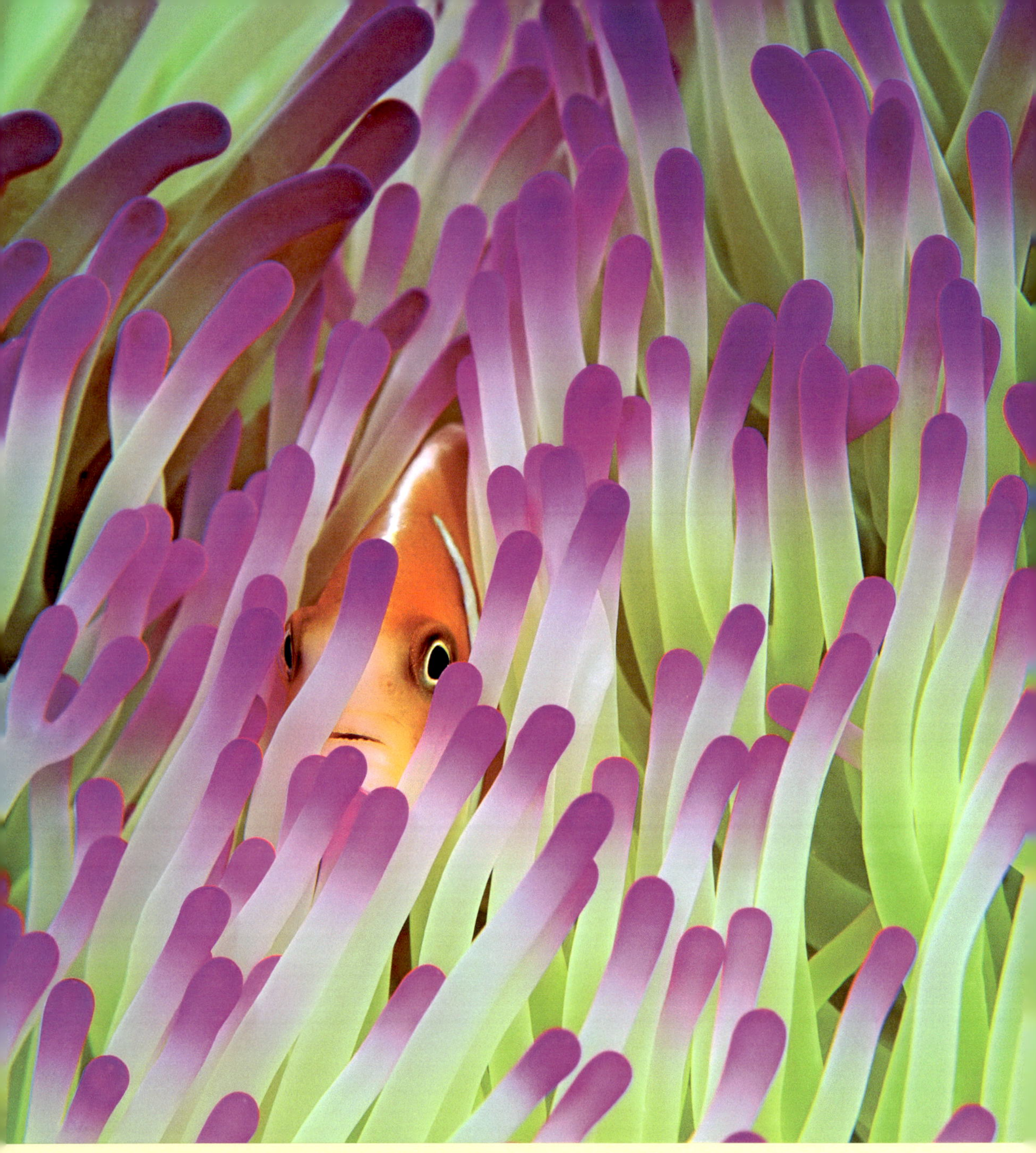

When you are sincere—when you "talk straight" with the Infinite—you will receive His response. You will see His magic presence playing hide-and-seek with you behind all the screens of material life. You will intuit His invisible power and beauty behind everything.

—Paramahansa Yogananda

Clownfish and anemones, Great Barrier Reef, Australia Photograph by Gary Bell/Oceanwide Images

February

22
monday

23
tuesday

24
wednesday

25
thursday

26
friday

Last Quarter ◑

27
saturday

28
sunday

FEBRUARY

S	M	T	W	T	F	S
	1	2	3	4	5	6
7	8	9	10	11	12	13
14	15	16	17	18	19	20
21	22	23	24	25	26	27
28						

MARCH

S	M	T	W	T	F	S
	1	2	3	4	5	6
7	8	9	10	11	12	13
14	15	16	17	18	19	20
21	22	23	24	25	26	27
28	29	30	31			

March

1
monday

2
tuesday

3
wednesday

4
thursday

5
friday

6
saturday

7
sunday

Paramahansa Yogananda's Mahasamadhi

MARCH

S	M	T	W	T	F	S
	1	2	3	4	5	6
7	8	9	10	11	12	13
14	15	16	17	18	19	20
21	22	23	24	25	26	27
28	29	30	31			

APRIL

S	M	T	W	T	F	S
				1	2	3
4	5	6	7	8	9	10
11	12	13	14	15	16	17
18	19	20	21	22	23	24
25	26	27	28	29	30	

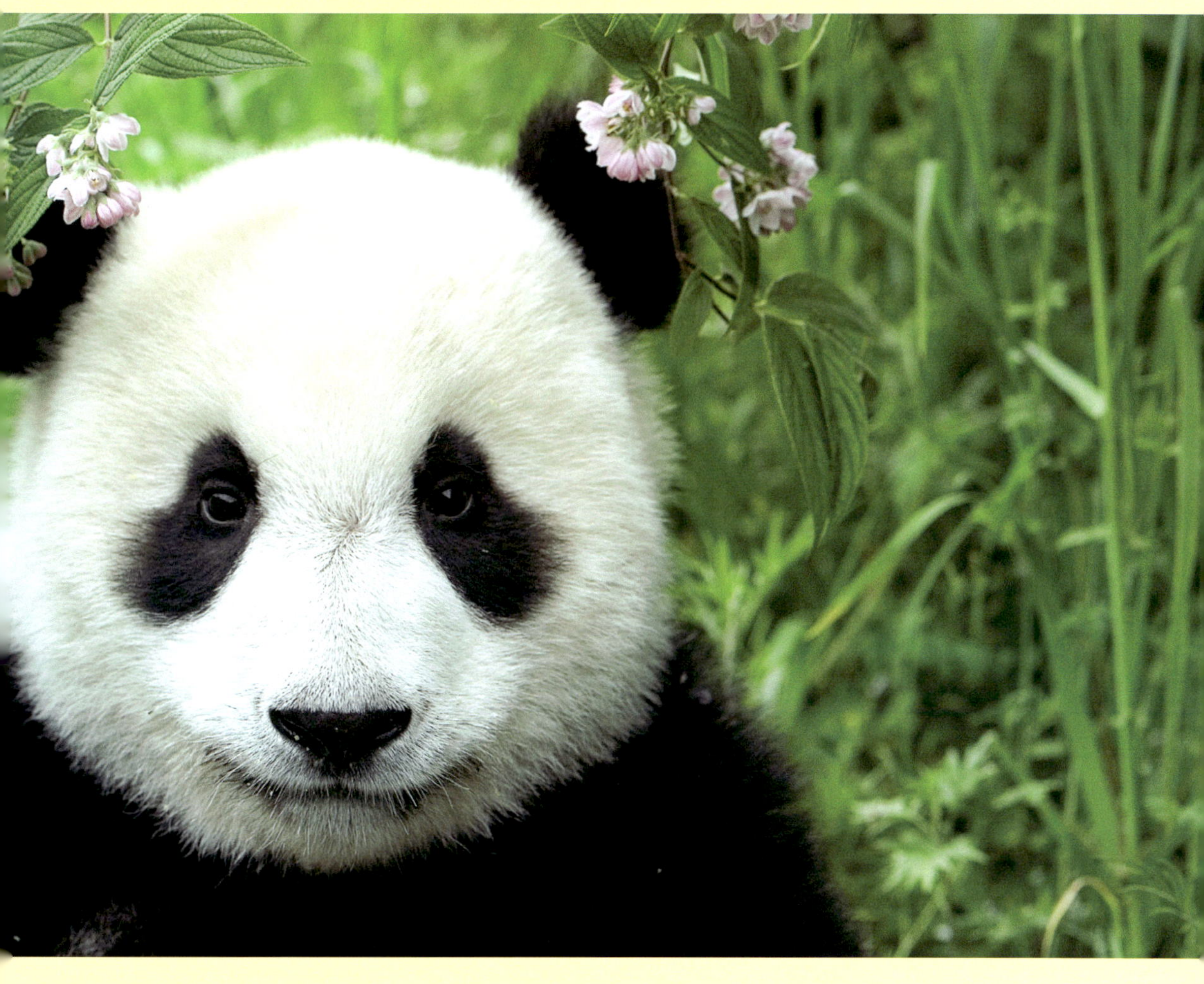

When your eyes become spiritually opened,
then you see the eyes of the Infinite looking at you
through the eyes of everyone you meet.

—Paramahansa Yogananda

Giant Panda, Wolong Giant Panda Garden, Sichuan, China   Photograph by Mitsuaki Iwago/Superstock

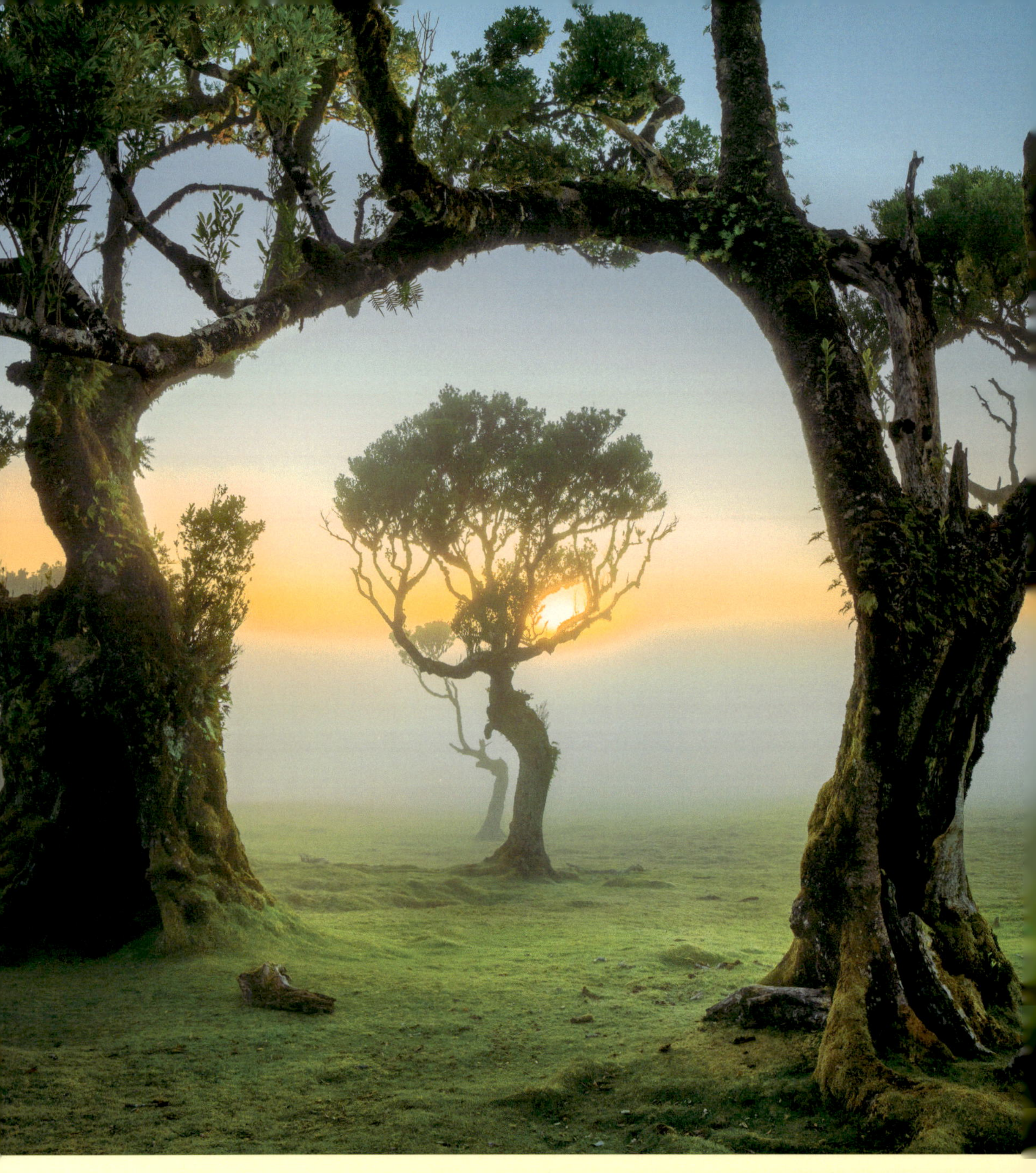

Divine Abundance follows the law of service and generosity. Give and then receive. Give to the world the best you have and the best will come back to you.

—Paramahansa Yogananda

Cloud Forest, Madeira Island, Portugal   Photograph by Daniel Kordan

March

New Moon ●

8
monday

Sri Yukteswar's Mahasamadhi

9
tuesday

10
wednesday

11
thursday

12
friday

13
saturday

Daylight Saving Time begins (U.S. and Canada)

14
sunday

MARCH

S	M	T	W	T	F	S
	1	2	3	4	5	6
7	8	9	10	11	12	13
14	15	16	17	18	19	20
21	22	23	24	25	26	27
28	29	30	31			

APRIL

S	M	T	W	T	F	S
				1	2	3
4	5	6	7	8	9	10
11	12	13	14	15	16	17
18	19	20	21	22	23	24
25	26	27	28	29	30	

March

15
monday

First Quarter ◐

16
tuesday

17
wednesday

St. Patrick's Day

18
thursday

19
friday

20
saturday

Vernal Equinox

21
sunday

March

S	M	T	W	T	F	S
	1	2	3	4	5	6
7	8	9	10	11	12	13
14	15	16	17	18	19	20
21	22	23	24	25	26	27
28	29	30	31			

April

S	M	T	W	T	F	S
				1	2	3
4	5	6	7	8	9	10
11	12	13	14	15	16	17
18	19	20	21	22	23	24
25	26	27	28	29	30	

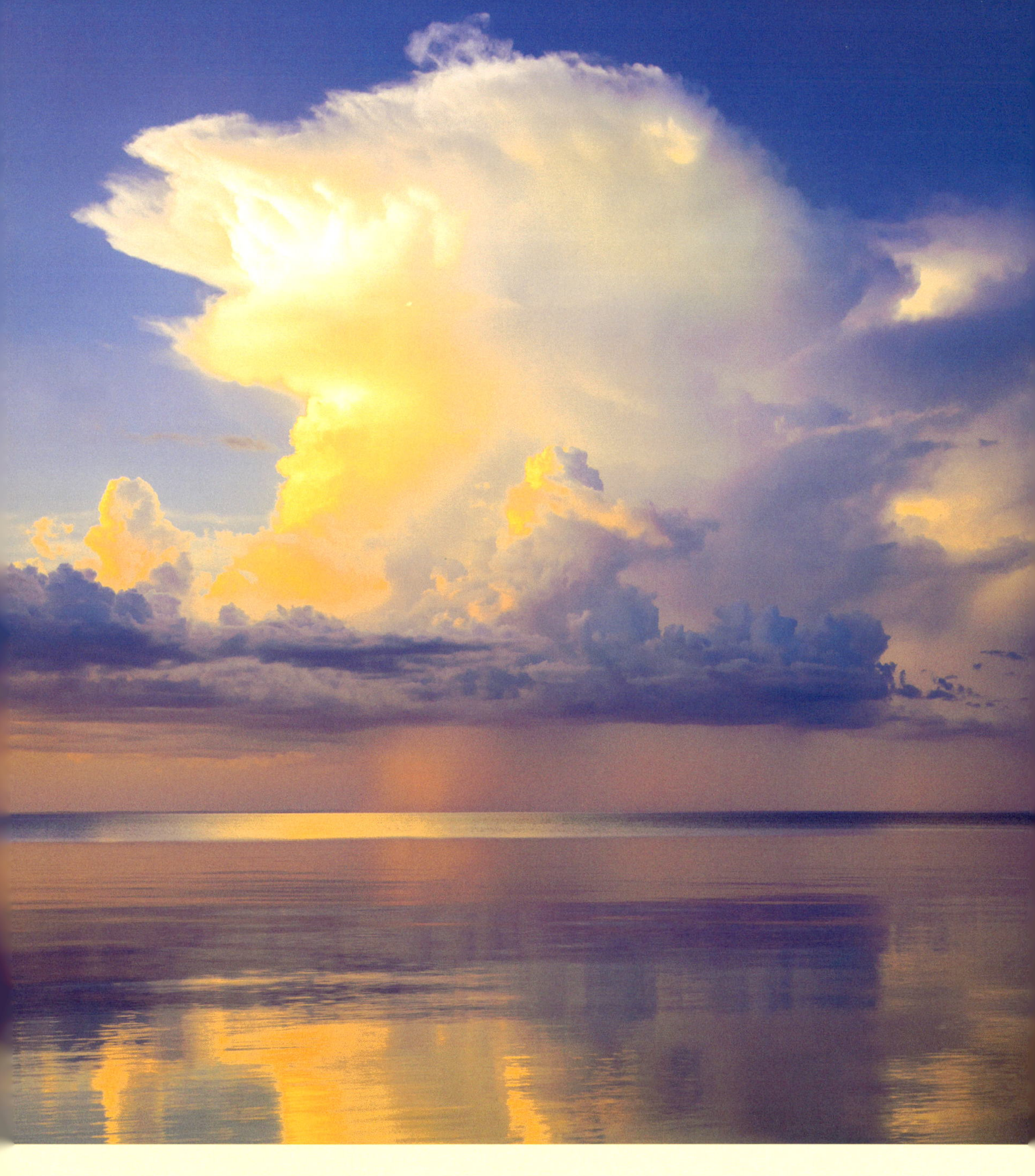

Imagination is a portal through which you can transcend
the imposed limitations of this world.

—Paramahansa Yogananda

Clouds over Lake Superior   Photograph by David Cobb

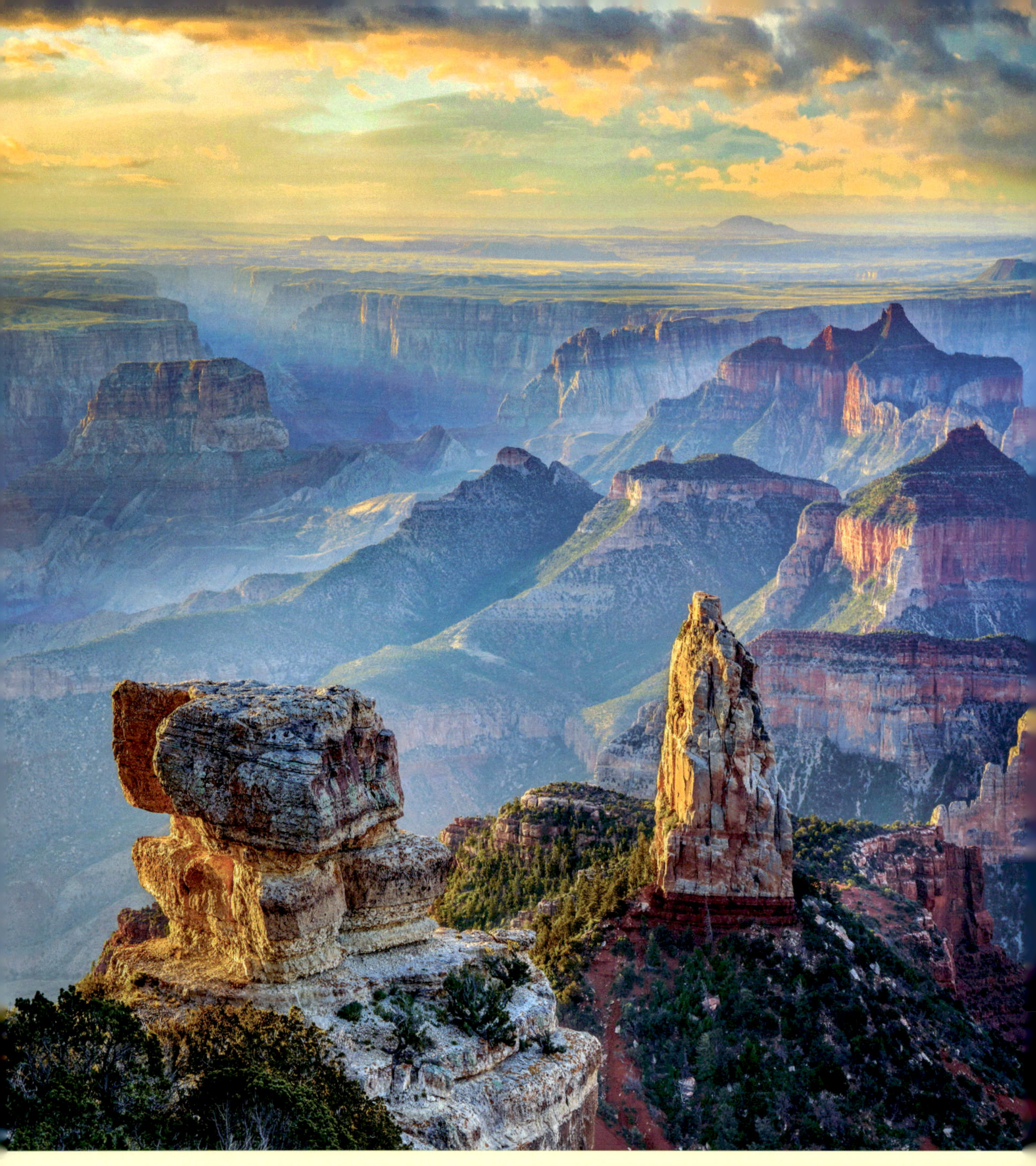

Only in the castle of God can we find protection.
There is no safer haven of joy than in His presence.
When you are with Him, nothing can touch you.

—Paramahansa Yogananda

Point Imperial, Grand Canyon National Park, Arizona Photograph by Tim Fitzharris

March

22
monday

Full Moon ○

23
tuesday

24
wednesday

25
thursday

26
friday

Good Friday

27
saturday

28
sunday

Easter Sunday Daylight Saving Time begins (U.K. and European Union)

MARCH

S	M	T	W	T	F	S
	1	2	3	4	5	6
7	8	9	10	11	12	13
14	15	16	17	18	19	20
21	22	23	24	25	26	27
28	29	30	31			

APRIL

S	M	T	W	T	F	S
				1	2	3
4	5	6	7	8	9	10
11	12	13	14	15	16	17
18	19	20	21	22	23	24
25	26	27	28	29	30	

March/April

29
monday

Easter Monday (All except U.S. and Scotland) Last Quarter ◑

30
tuesday

31
wednesday

1
thursday

2
friday

3
saturday

4
sunday

March

S	M	T	W	T	F	S
	1	2	3	4	5	6
7	8	9	10	11	12	13
14	15	16	17	18	19	20
21	22	23	24	25	26	27
28	29	30	31			

April

S	M	T	W	T	F	S
				1	2	3
4	5	6	7	8	9	10
11	12	13	14	15	16	17
18	19	20	21	22	23	24
25	26	27	28	29	30	

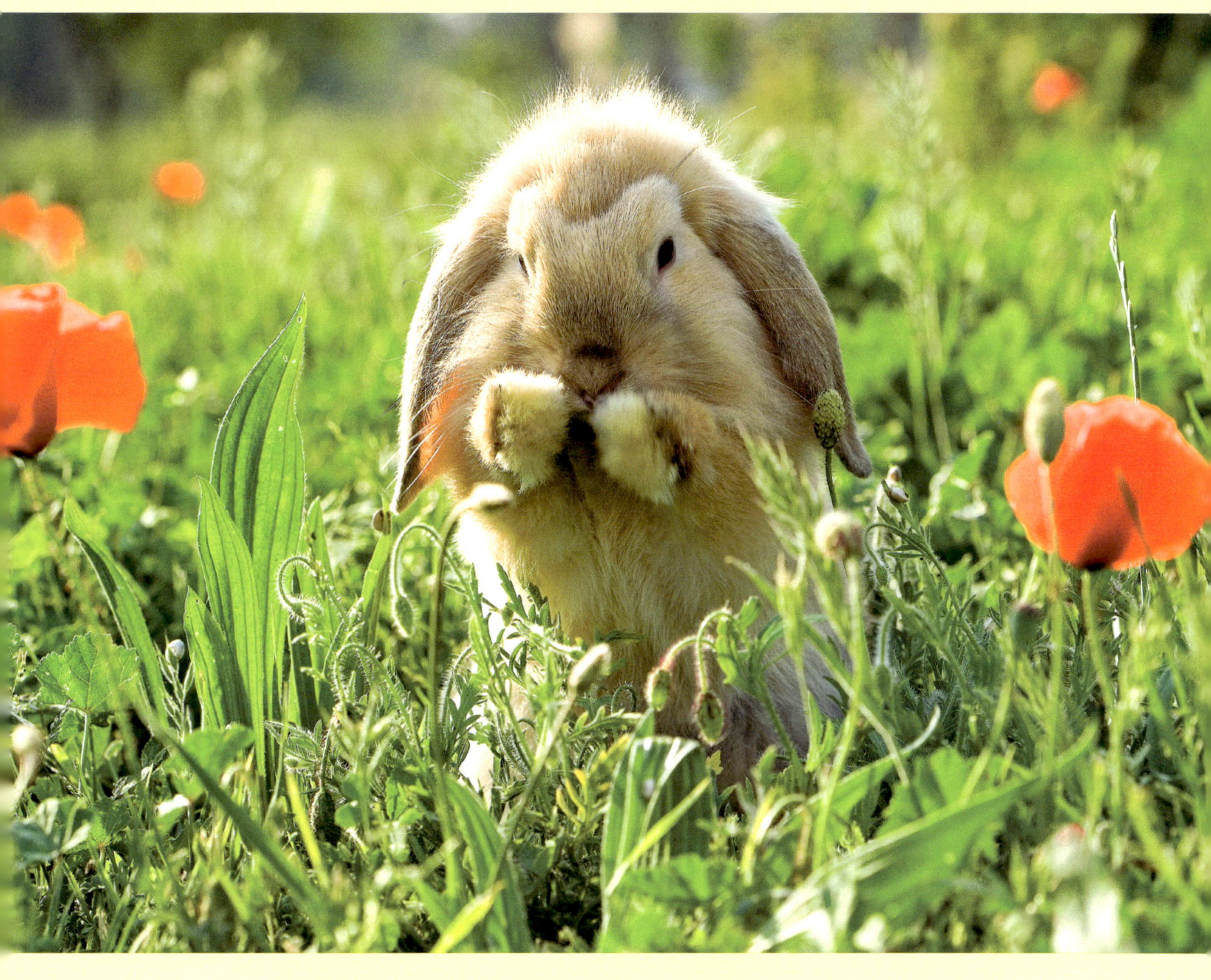

Those who live in tune with the attractive force of love achieve harmony with nature and their fellow beings.

—Paramahansa Yogananda

Dwarf Lop-eared Rabbit in spring meadow, France Photograph by Michel Gunther/Superstock

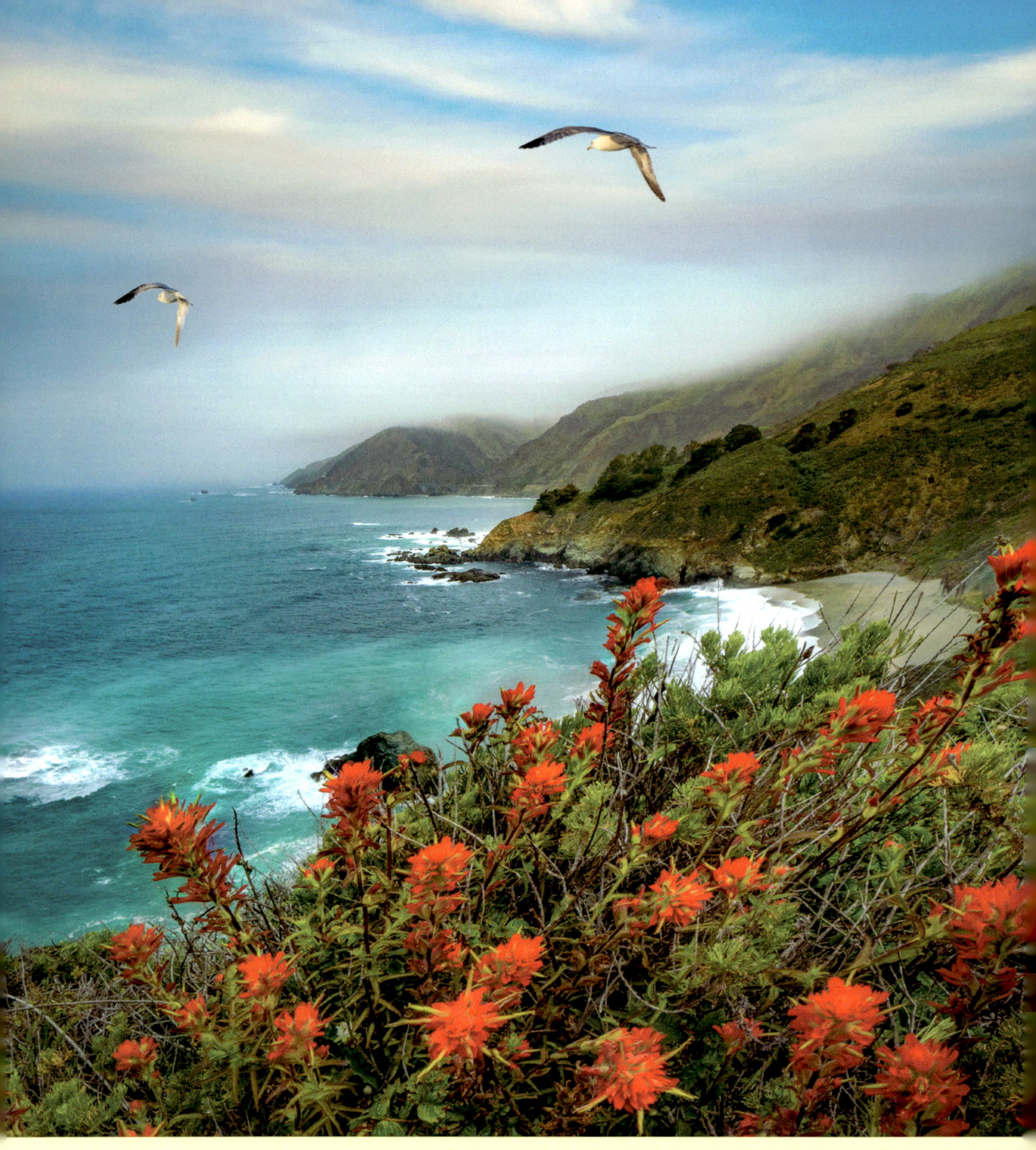

By meditation rise above everything; see God as oneness within, then project that oneness by loving your family, nation, world, all creatures, all planets as one Spirit.

—Paramahansa Yogananda

Big Sur, California Photograph by Tim Fitzharris

April

5
monday

6
tuesday

New Moon ●

7
wednesday

8
thursday

9
friday

APRIL

S	M	T	W	T	F	S
				1	2	3
4	5	6	7	8	9	10
11	12	13	14	15	16	17
18	19	20	21	22	23	24
25	26	27	28	29	30	

MAY

S	M	T	W	T	F	S
						1
2	3	4	5	6	7	8
9	10	11	12	13	14	15
16	17	18	19	20	21	22
23/30	24/31	25	26	27	28	29

10
saturday

11
sunday

April

12
monday

13
tuesday

First Quarter ◐

14
wednesday

15
thursday

16
friday

17
saturday

18
sunday

April

S	M	T	W	T	F	S
				1	2	3
4	5	6	7	8	9	10
11	12	13	14	15	16	17
18	19	20	21	22	23	24
25	26	27	28	29	30	

May

S	M	T	W	T	F	S
						1
2	3	4	5	6	7	8
9	10	11	12	13	14	15
16	17	18	19	20	21	22
23/30	24/31	25	26	27	28	29

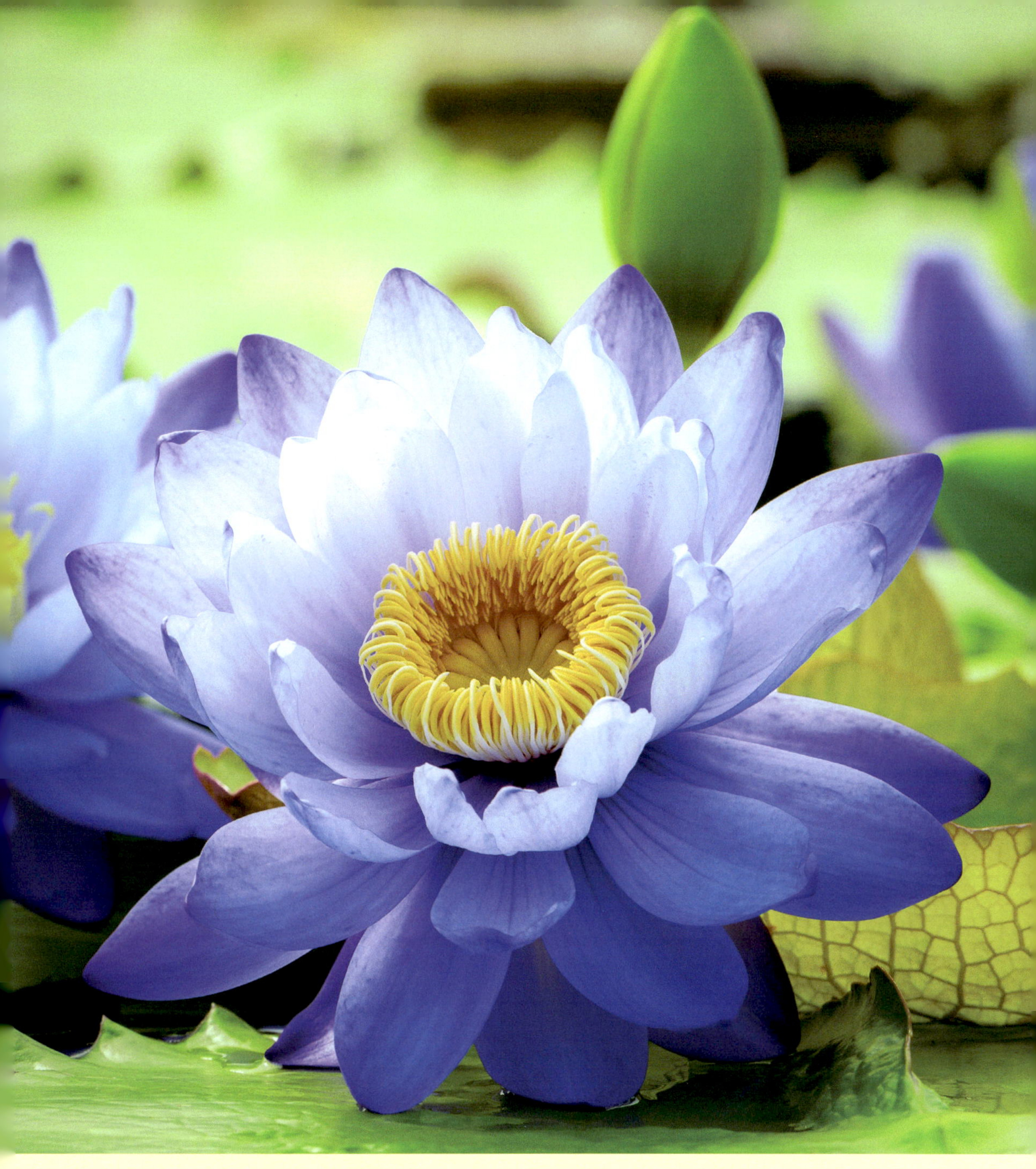

As I radiate love and goodwill to others,
I will open the channel for God's love to come to me.
Divine love is the magnet that draws to me all good.

—Paramahansa Yogananda

Water lily pond near Stuttgart, Germany   Photograph by Lilly/Superstock

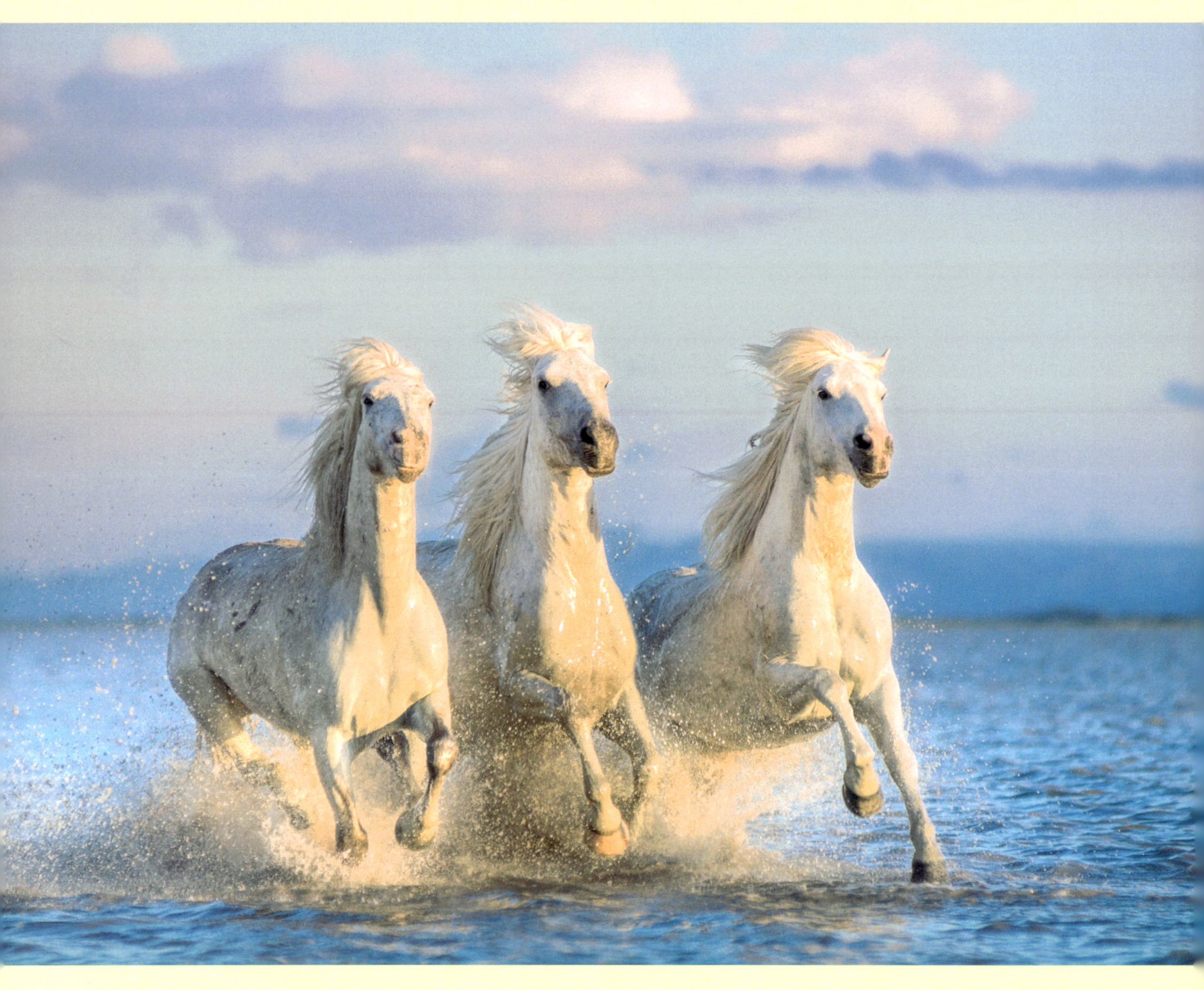

When perfect friendship exists either between two hearts or within a group of hearts...such friendship perfects each individual. The heart purified by friendship provides an open door to unity.

—Paramahansa Yogananda

Wild horses of the Camargue, Southern France   Photograph by Daniel Kordan

April

19
monday

Full Moon ○

20
tuesday

Passover begins

21
wednesday

22
thursday

23
friday

April

S	M	T	W	T	F	S
				1	2	3
4	5	6	7	8	9	10
11	12	13	14	15	16	17
18	19	20	21	22	23	24
25	26	27	28	29	30	

24
saturday

May

S	M	T	W	T	F	S
						1
2	3	4	5	6	7	8
9	10	11	12	13	14	15
16	17	18	19	20	21	22
23/30	24/31	25	26	27	28	29

25
sunday

April/May

26
monday

27
tuesday

28
wednesday

Last Quarter ◑

29
thursday

30
friday

1
saturday

2
sunday

April

S	M	T	W	T	F	S
				1	2	3
4	5	6	7	8	9	10
11	12	13	14	15	16	17
18	19	20	21	22	23	24
25	26	27	28	29	30	

May

S	M	T	W	T	F	S
						1
2	3	4	5	6	7	8
9	10	11	12	13	14	15
16	17	18	19	20	21	22
23/30	24/31	25	26	27	28	29

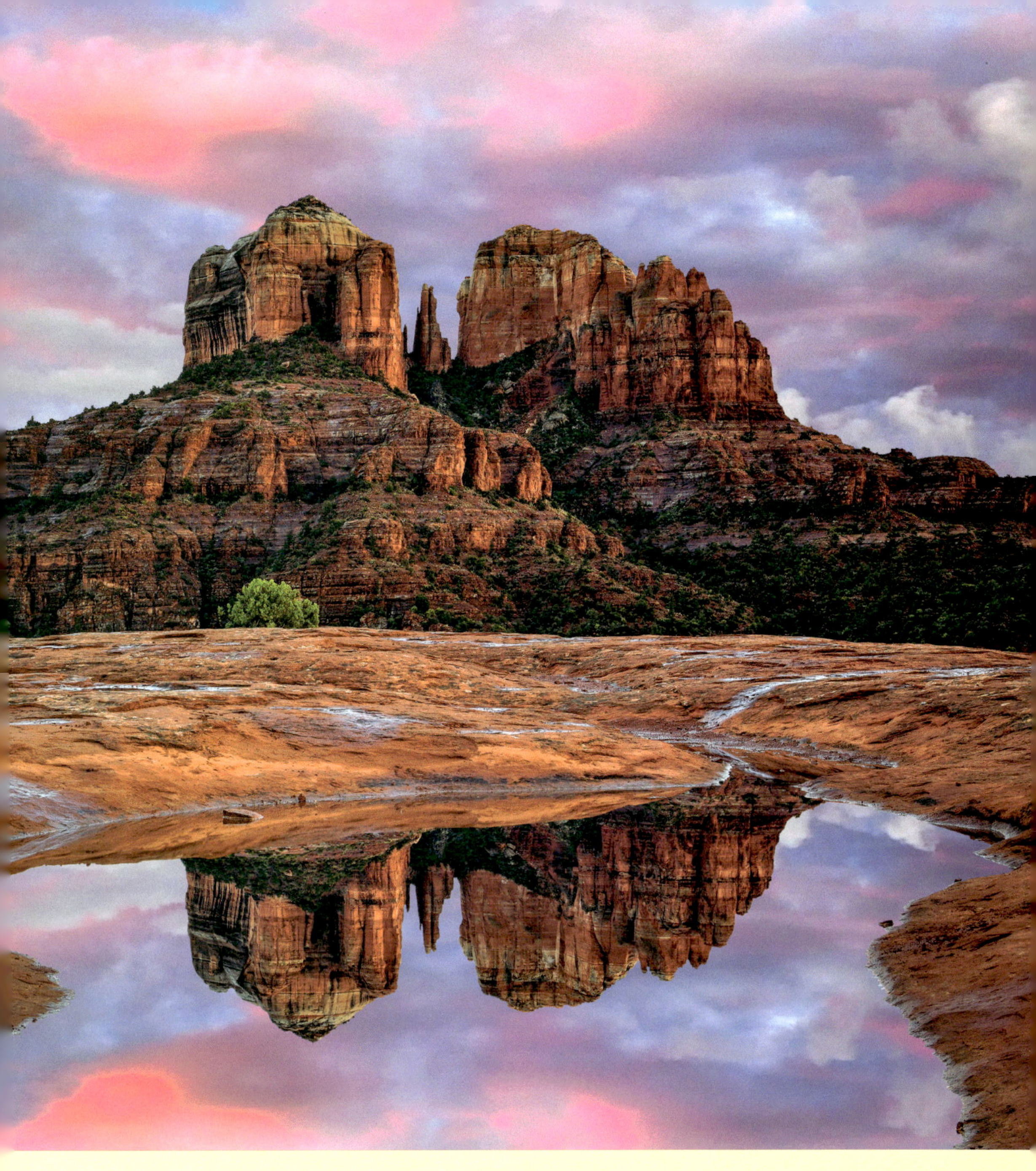

On the throne of silent thoughts the God of peace
is directing my actions today.

—Paramahansa Yogananda

Cathedral Rock, Sedona, Arizona Photograph by Dean Hueber

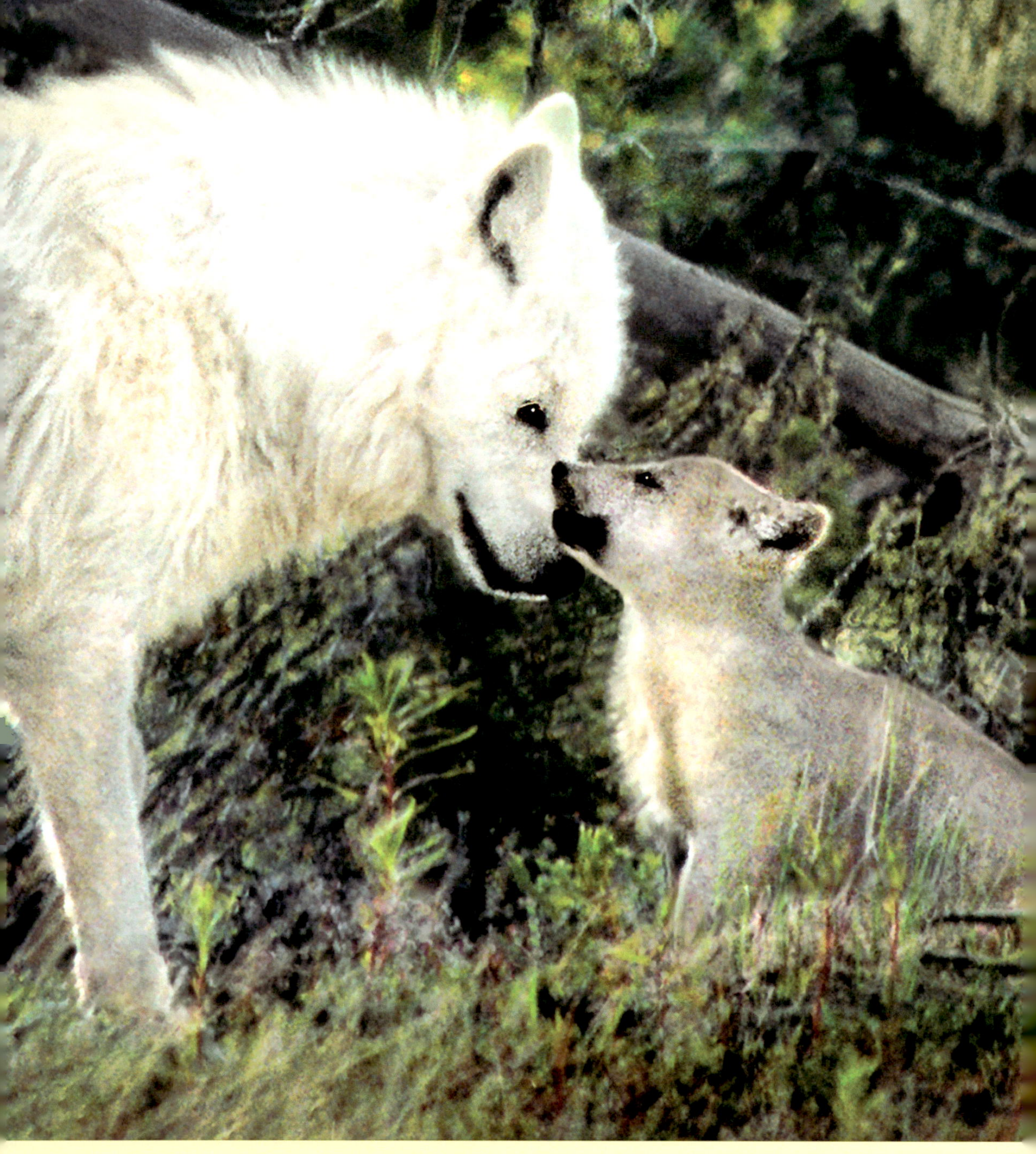

The mother's love is not given to us to spoil us with indulgence,
but to soften our hearts, that we may in turn soften others with kindness.

—Paramahansa Yogananda

Mother wolf and pup, Northwest Territories, Canada   Photograph by Dave Welling

May

3
monday

4
tuesday

5
wednesday

National Day of Prayer New Moon ●

6
thursday

7
friday

8
saturday

Mother's Day (U.S., Canada, Australia, N.Z.)

9
sunday

MAY

S	M	T	W	T	F	S
						1
2	3	4	5	6	7	8
9	10	11	12	13	14	15
16	17	18	19	20	21	22
23/30	24/31	25	26	27	28	29

JUNE

S	M	T	W	T	F	S
		1	2	3	4	5
6	7	8	9	10	11	12
13	14	15	16	17	18	19
20	21	22	23	24	25	26
27	28	29	30			

May

10
monday

Sri Yukteswar's Birthday

11
tuesday

12
wednesday

First Quarter ◐

13
thursday

14
friday

15
saturday

16
sunday

May

S	M	T	W	T	F	S
						1
2	3	4	5	6	7	8
9	10	11	12	13	14	15
16	17	18	19	20	21	22
23/30	24/31	25	26	27	28	29

June

S	M	T	W	T	F	S
		1	2	3	4	5
6	7	8	9	10	11	12
13	14	15	16	17	18	19
20	21	22	23	24	25	26
27	28	29	30			

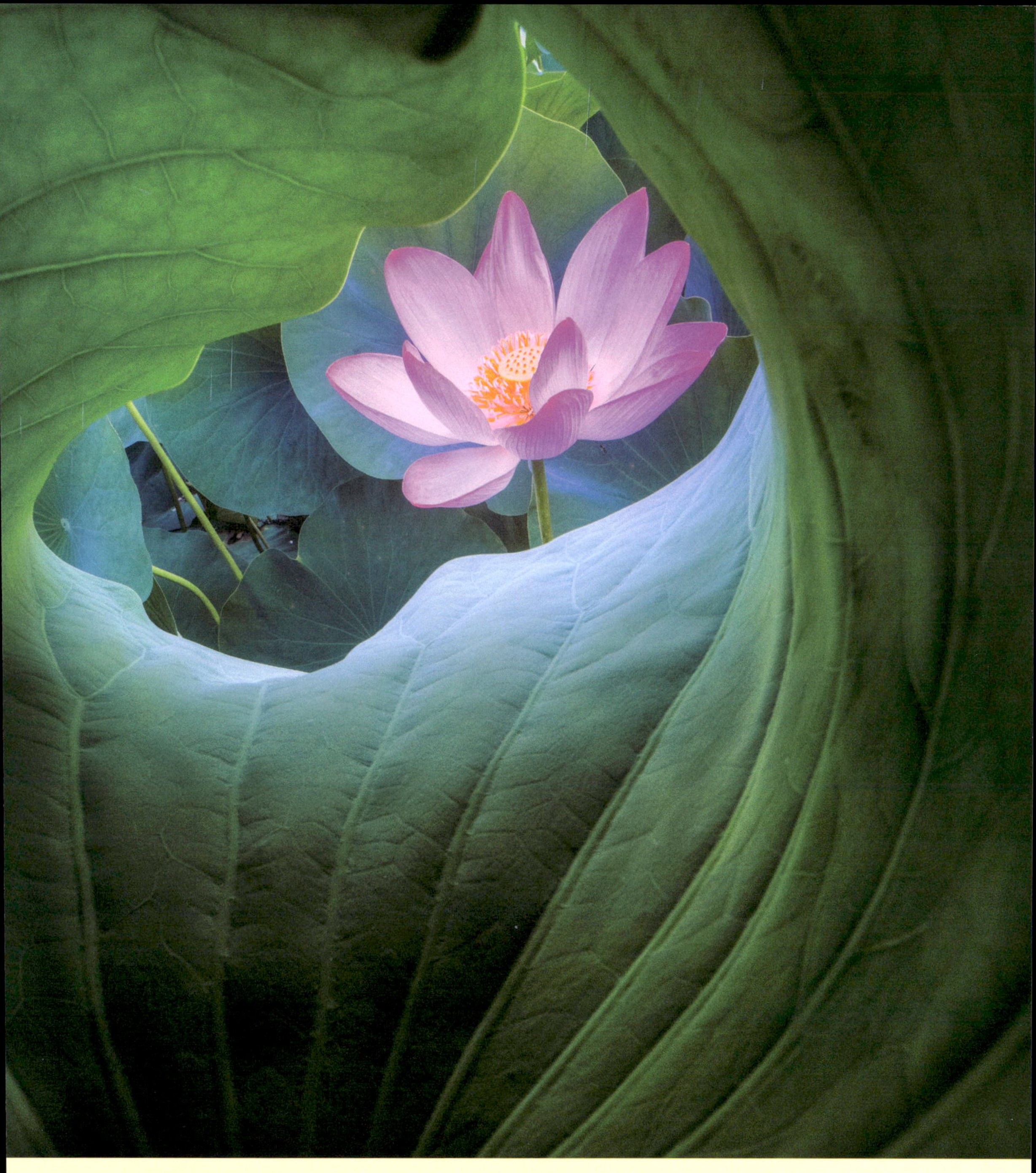

God is in the heart and soul of every being. And when you open within yourself the secret temple in your heart, then with the all-knowing intuition of the soul you shall read the book of life.

—Paramahansa Yogananda

Lotus flower, Mekong Delta, Vietnam   Photograph by Daniel Kordan

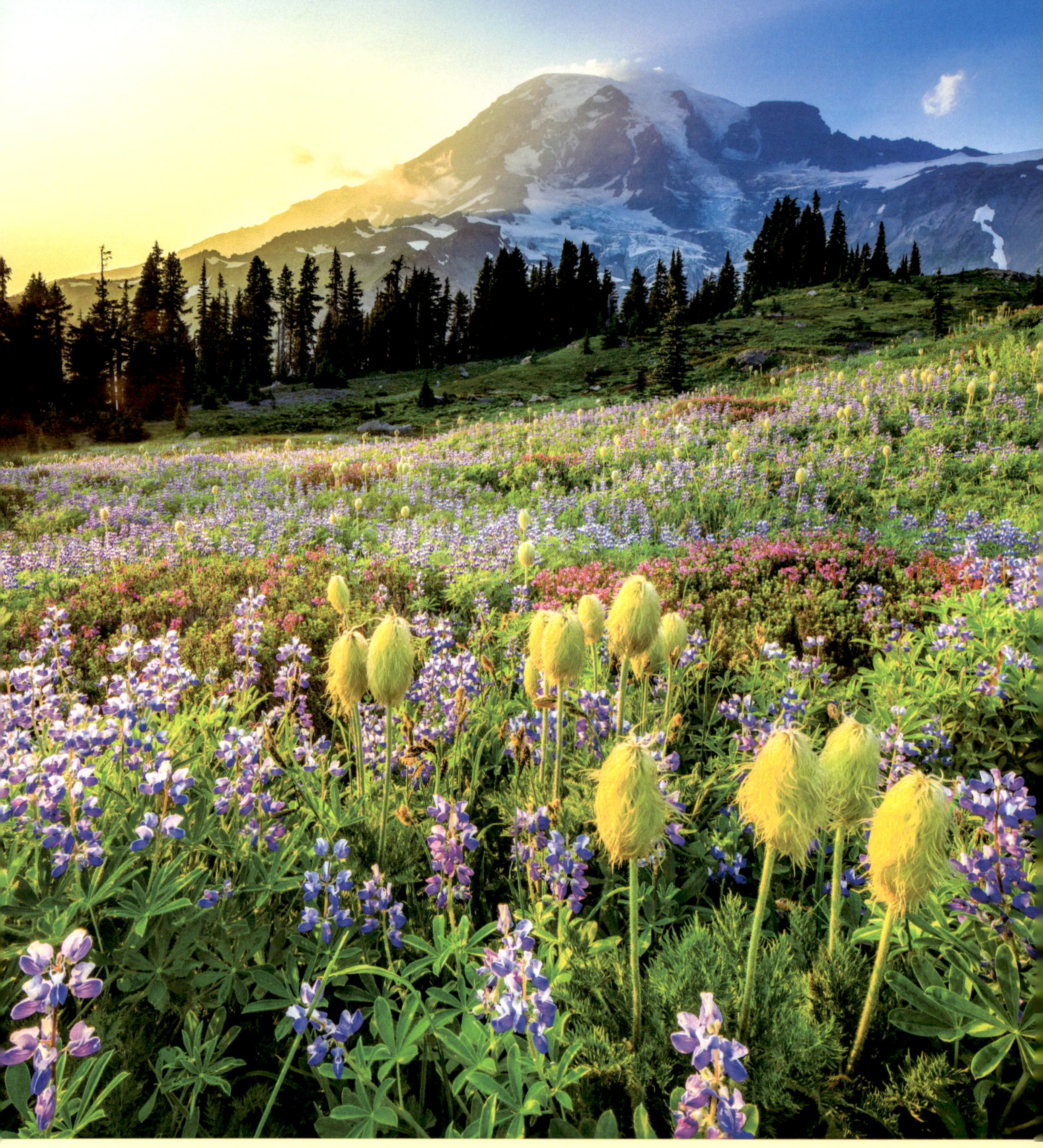

The love of God, the love of the Spirit, is an all-consuming love. Once you have experienced it, it shall lead you on and on in the eternal realms. That love will never be taken away from your heart.

—Paramahansa Yogananda

Mount Rainier National Park, Washington Photograph by Alan Majchrowicz

May

17
monday

18
tuesday

19
wednesday

Full Moon ○

20
thursday

21
friday

MAY

S	M	T	W	T	F	S
						1
2	3	4	5	6	7	8
9	10	11	12	13	14	15
16	17	18	19	20	21	22
23/30	24/31	25	26	27	28	29

22
saturday

JUNE

S	M	T	W	T	F	S
		1	2	3	4	5
6	7	8	9	10	11	12
13	14	15	16	17	18	19
20	21	22	23	24	25	26
27	28	29	30			

23
sunday

May

24
monday

Victoria Day (Canada)

25
tuesday

26
wednesday

27
thursday

28
friday

Last Quarter ◑

29
saturday

30
sunday

MAY

S	M	T	W	T	F	S
						1
2	3	4	5	6	7	8
9	10	11	12	13	14	15
16	17	18	19	20	21	22
23/30	24/31	25	26	27	28	29

JUNE

S	M	T	W	T	F	S
		1	2	3	4	5
6	7	8	9	10	11	12
13	14	15	16	17	18	19
20	21	22	23	24	25	26
27	28	29	30			

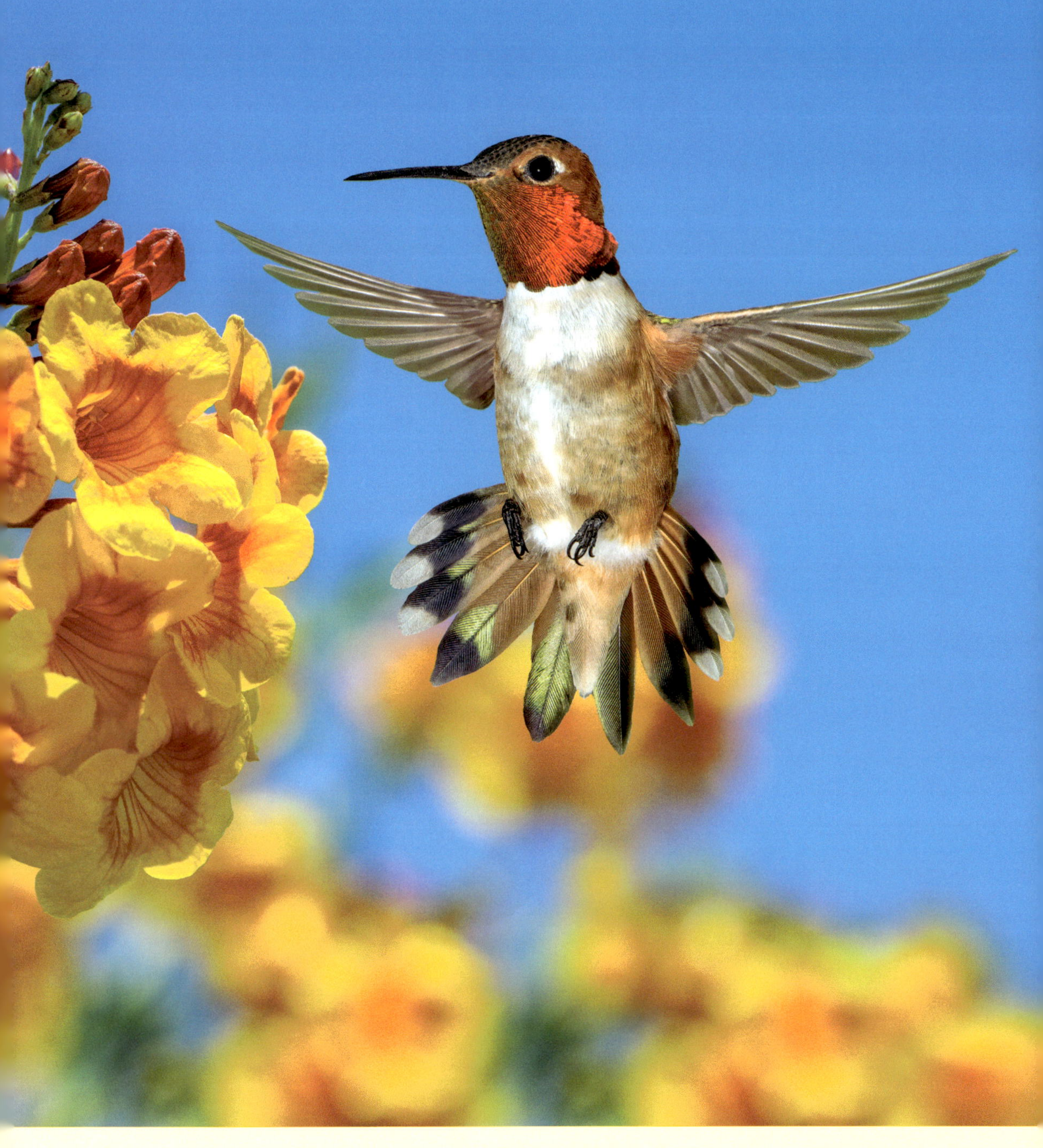

Always listen to your conscience, the voice of your inner self;
it is there to help you get along with yourself.

—Paramahansa Yogananda

Rufous Hummingbird and Trumpet Vine, Greer, Arizona   Photograph by Dean Hueber

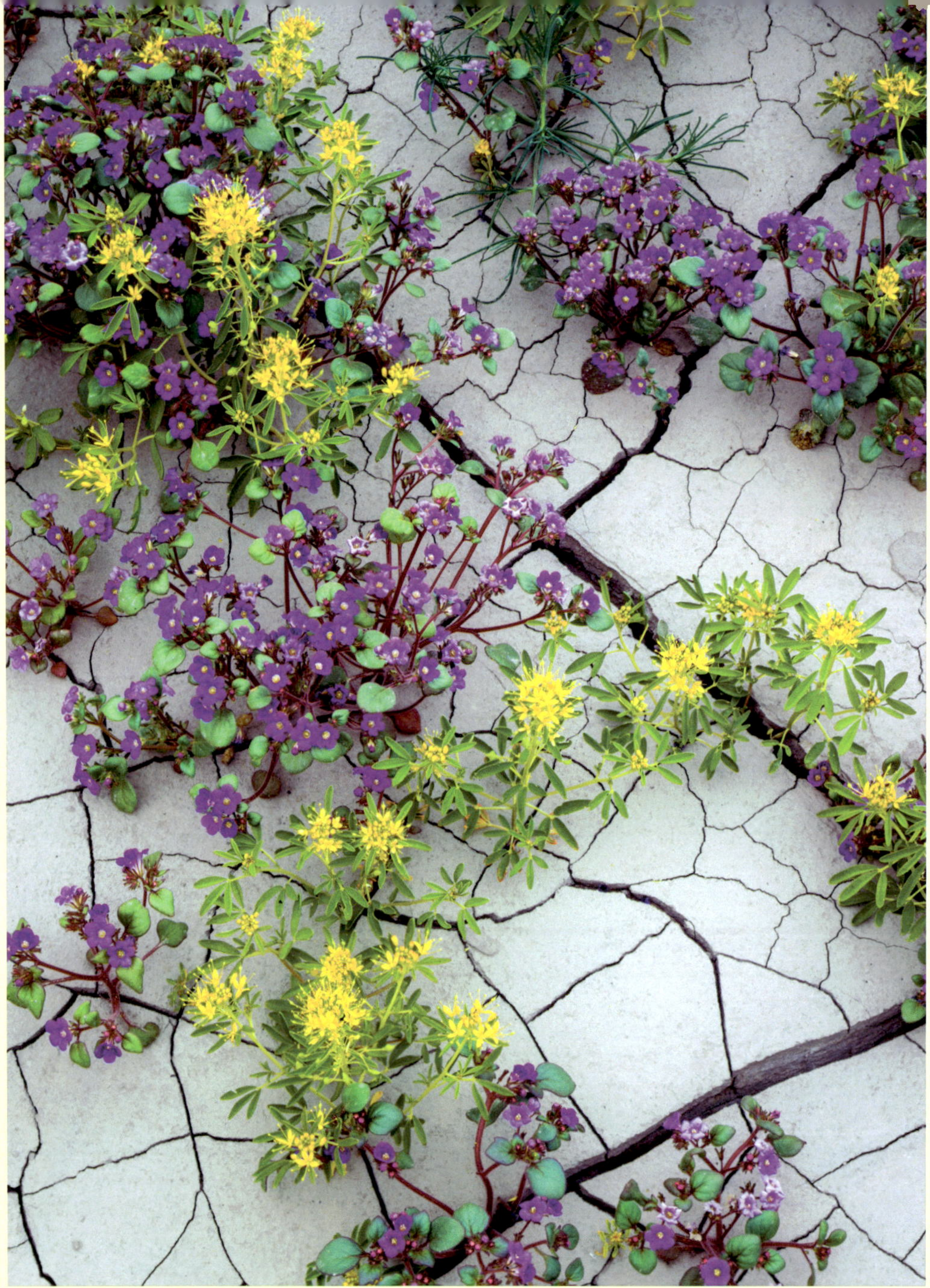

Whatever you want to accomplish, affirm and believe in its attainment, in spite of contrary evidence. Create the pattern of success in your subconscious mind and make it work for you.

—Paramahansa Yogananda

Phacelia and Yellow Bee flowers, near Factory Butte, Utah   Photograph by Scott T. Smith

May/June

31
monday

Memorial Day

1
tuesday

2
wednesday

3
thursday

4
friday

New Moon ●

5
saturday

6
sunday

MAY

S	M	T	W	T	F	S
						1
2	3	4	5	6	7	8
9	10	11	12	13	14	15
16	17	18	19	20	21	22
23/30	24/31	25	26	27	28	29

JUNE

S	M	T	W	T	F	S
		1	2	3	4	5
6	7	8	9	10	11	12
13	14	15	16	17	18	19
20	21	22	23	24	25	26
27	28	29	30			

June

7
monday

8
tuesday

9
wednesday

10
thursday

11
friday

First Quarter ◐

12
saturday

13
sunday

June

S	M	T	W	T	F	S
		1	2	3	4	5
6	7	8	9	10	11	12
13	14	15	16	17	18	19
20	21	22	23	24	25	26
27	28	29	30			

July

S	M	T	W	T	F	S
				1	2	3
4	5	6	7	8	9	10
11	12	13	14	15	16	17
18	19	20	21	22	23	24
25	26	27	28	29	30	31

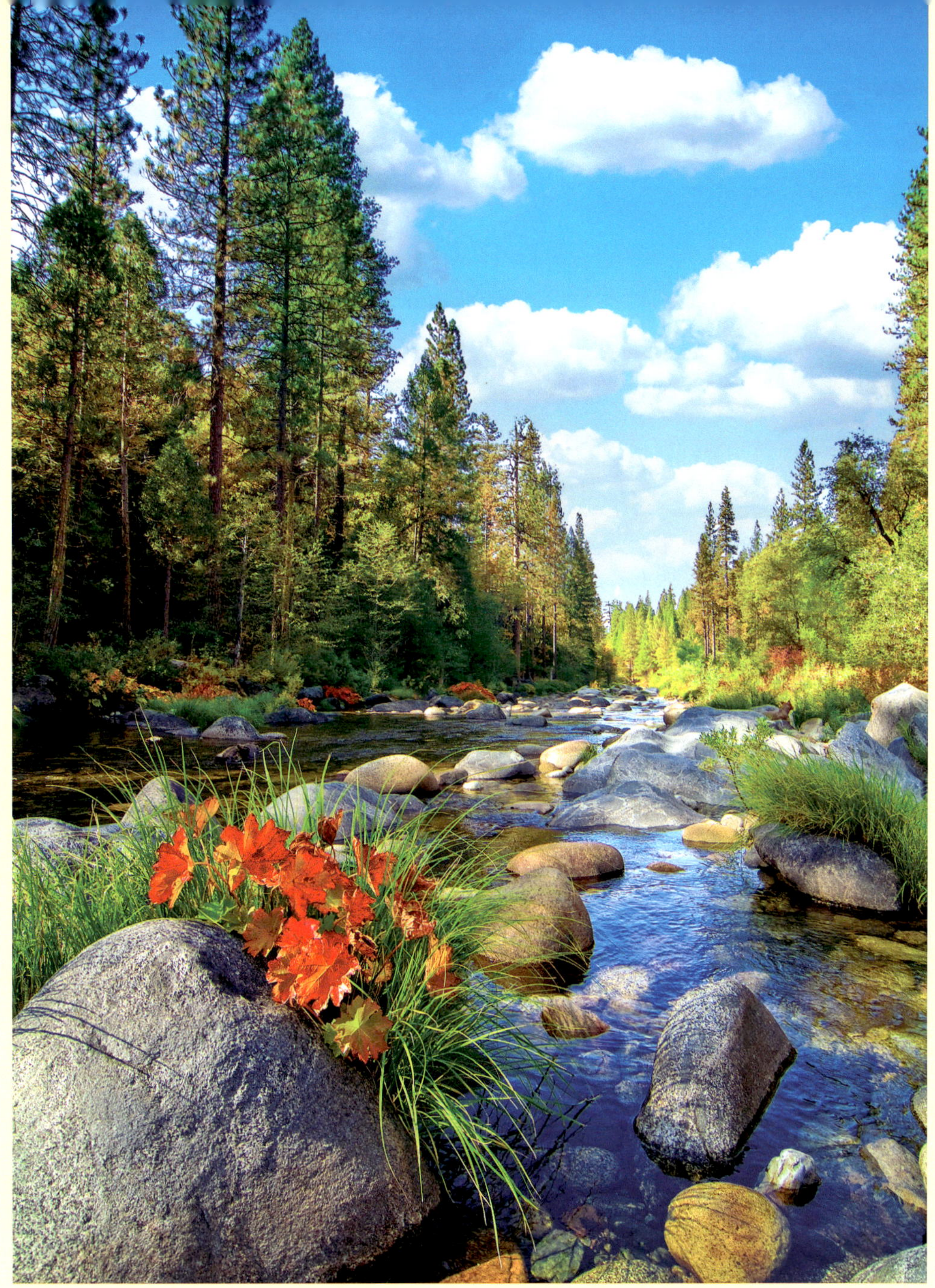

Every noble thought in your mind brings you closer to God.
Those thoughts are like a river leading to the ocean of Spirit.

—Paramahansa Yogananda

Yosemite National Park, California Photograph by Bunny Abrams

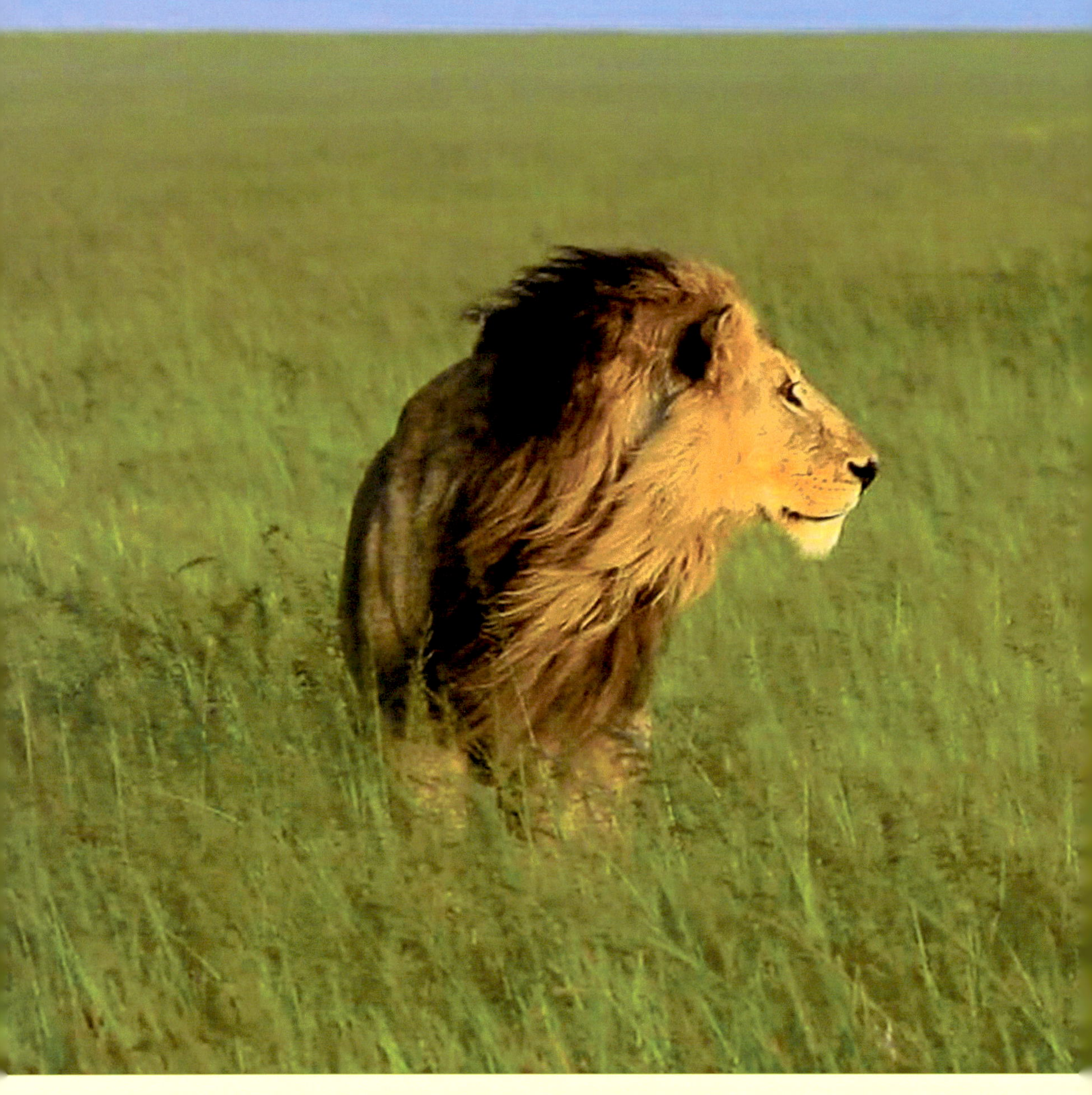

Seek quiet places where you can regularly get away by yourself
and be free to think of God.

—Paramahansa Yogananda

Male lion, Serengeti National Park, Tanzania Photograph by Boyd Norton

June

14
monday

15
tuesday

16
wednesday

17
thursday

Full Moon ○

18
friday

JUNE

S	M	T	W	T	F	S
		1	2	3	4	5
6	7	8	9	10	11	12
13	14	15	16	17	18	19
20	21	22	23	24	25	26
27	28	29	30			

JULY

S	M	T	W	T	F	S
				1	2	3
4	5	6	7	8	9	10
11	12	13	14	15	16	17
18	19	20	21	22	23	24
25	26	27	28	29	30	31

Juneteenth

19
saturday

Father's Day (U.S., Canada, U.K.)

20
sunday

June

21
monday

UN International Day of Yoga — Summer Solstice

22
tuesday

23
wednesday

24
thursday

25
friday

26
saturday

Last Quarter ◑

27
sunday

JUNE

S	M	T	W	T	F	S
		1	2	3	4	5
6	7	8	9	10	11	12
13	14	15	16	17	18	19
20	21	22	23	24	25	26
27	28	29	30			

JULY

S	M	T	W	T	F	S
				1	2	3
4	5	6	7	8	9	10
11	12	13	14	15	16	17
18	19	20	21	22	23	24
25	26	27	28	29	30	31

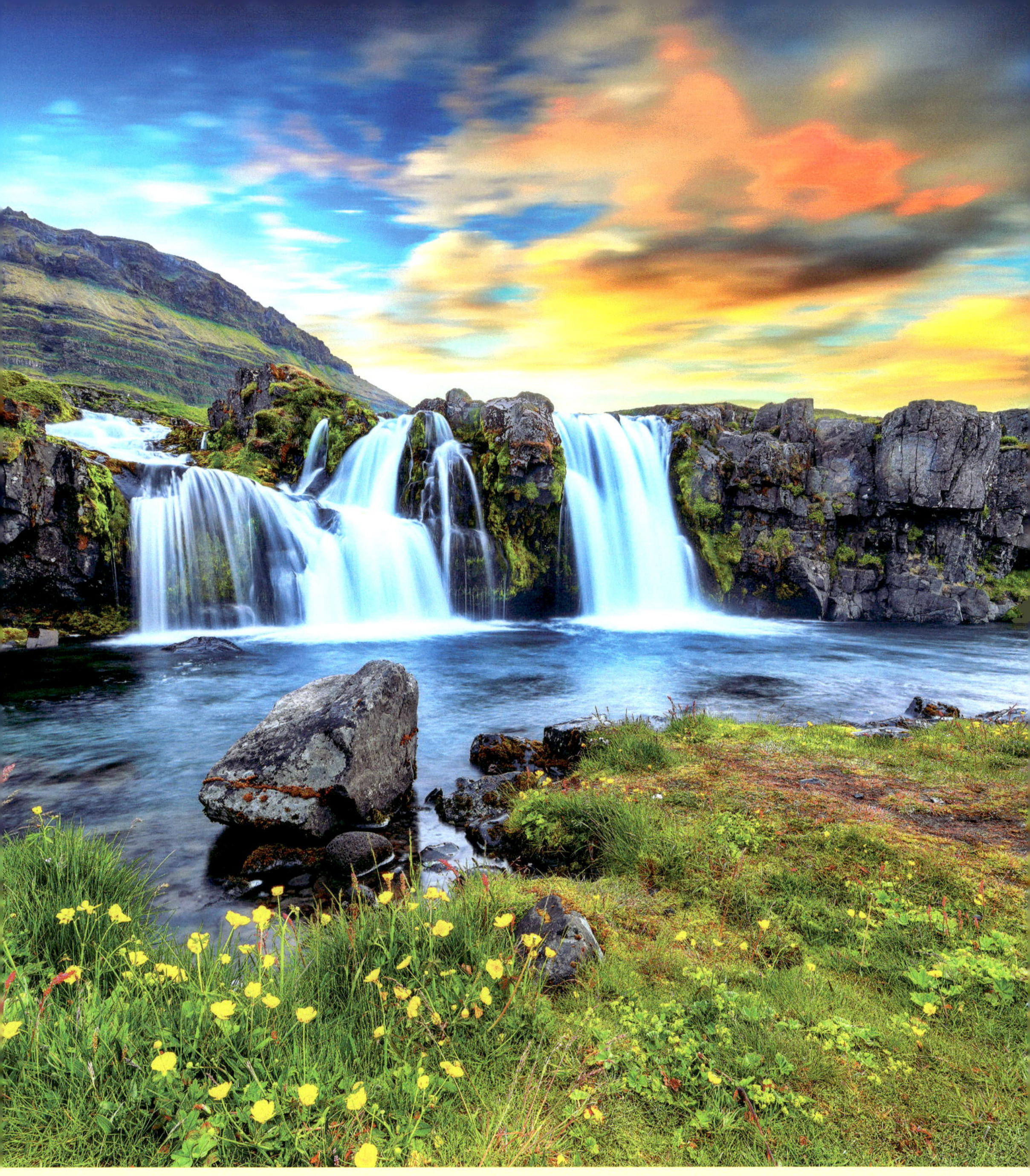

The soul cannot be confined within man-made boundaries.
Its nationality is Spirit; its country is Omnipresence.

—Paramahansa Yogananda

Kirkjufellsfoss, Iceland   Photograph by Vadym Lavra

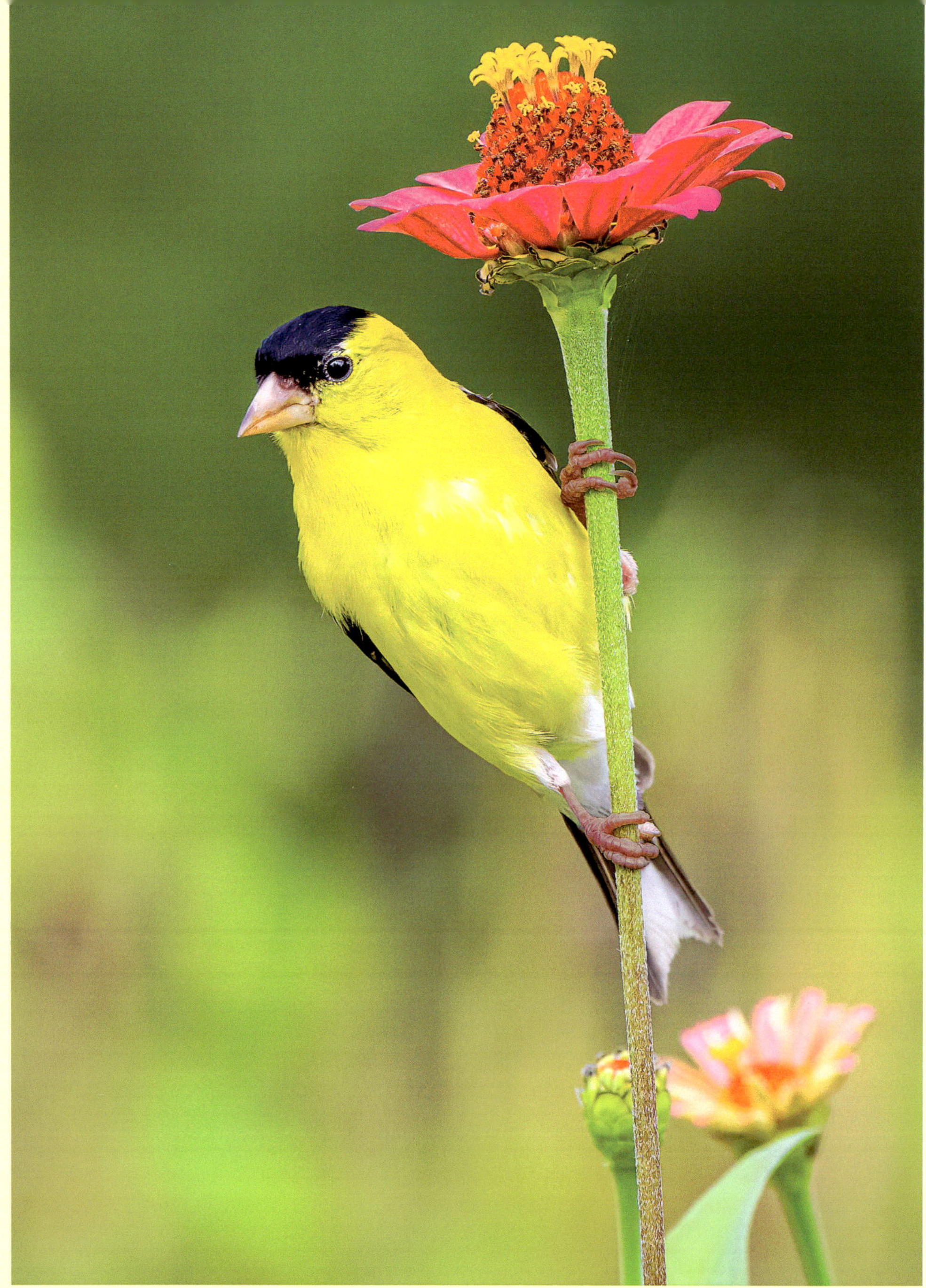

Condition your conscious mind power to watch for opportunities—to recognize the little openings that take you where you want to go, and to seize those opportunities that are consistent with your goals.

—Paramahansa Yogananda

American Goldfinch, Marion County, Illinois Photograph by Richard Day

June/July

28
monday

29
tuesday

30
wednesday

Canada Day (Canada)

1
thursday

2
friday

JUNE

S	M	T	W	T	F	S
		1	2	3	4	5
6	7	8	9	10	11	12
13	14	15	16	17	18	19
20	21	22	23	24	25	26
27	28	29	30			

JULY

S	M	T	W	T	F	S
				1	2	3
4	5	6	7	8	9	10
11	12	13	14	15	16	17
18	19	20	21	22	23	24
25	26	27	28	29	30	31

New Moon ●

3
saturday

Independence Day

4
sunday

July

5
monday

6
tuesday

7
wednesday

8
thursday

9
friday

10
saturday

First Quarter ◐

11
sunday

July

S	M	T	W	T	F	S
				1	2	3
4	5	6	7	8	9	10
11	12	13	14	15	16	17
18	19	20	21	22	23	24
25	26	27	28	29	30	31

August

S	M	T	W	T	F	S
1	2	3	4	5	6	7
8	9	10	11	12	13	14
15	16	17	18	19	20	21
22	23	24	25	26	27	28
29	30	31				

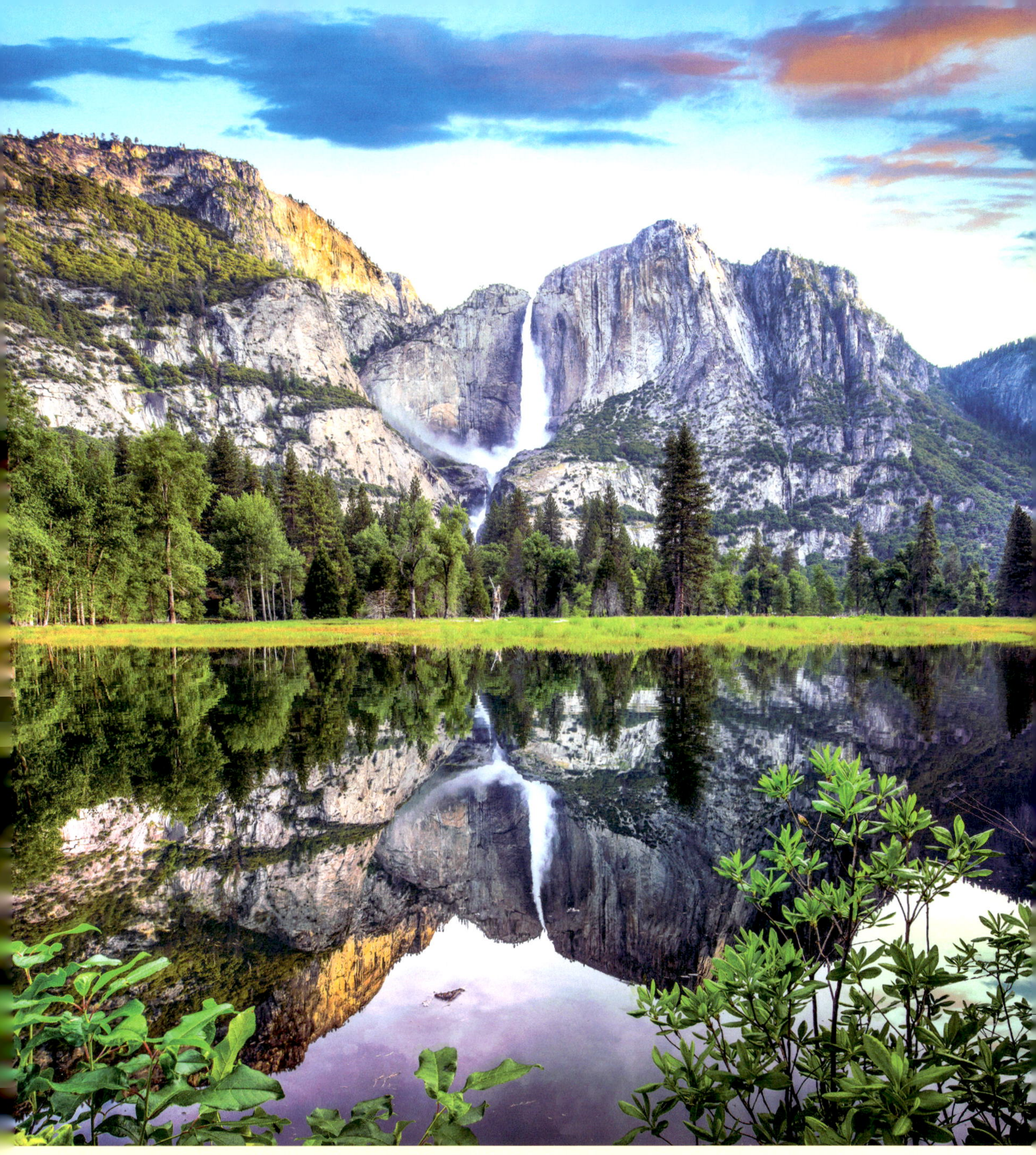

Calm all restlessness of body and mind so that you can see the clear reflection of the soul mirrored in the unruffled lake of your consciousness.

—Paramahansa Yogananda

Yosemite National Park, California Photograph by Tim Fitzharris

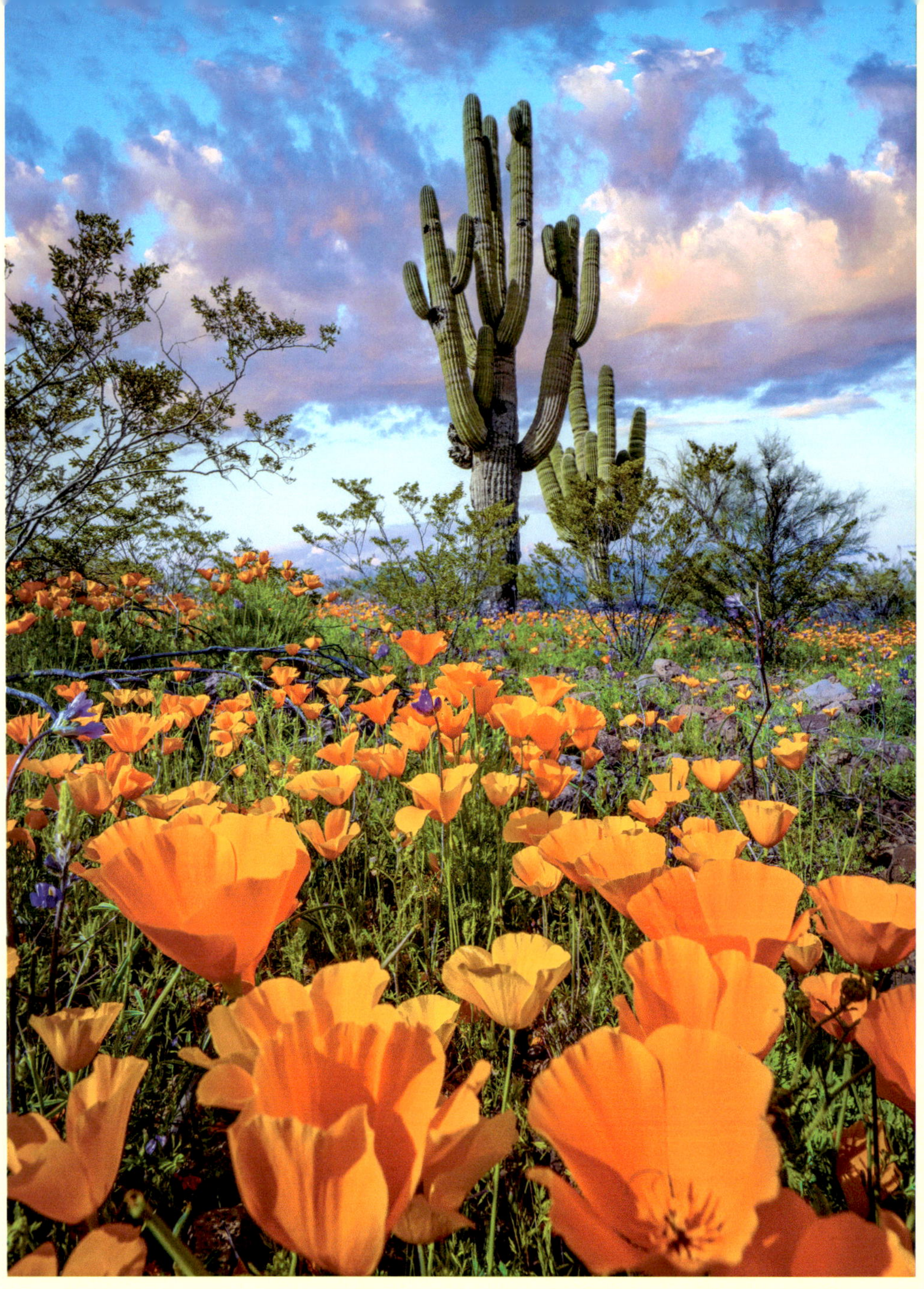

God says, "Follow the trail of beauty. I am hidden somewhere in its heart.
I am Harmony, I am Love, I am Beauty,
I am Fragrance, I am Joy."

—Paramahansa Yogananda

California Poppies, Peridot Mesa, Arizona Photograph by Tim Fitzharris

July

12
monday

13
tuesday

14
wednesday

15
thursday

16
friday

JULY

S	M	T	W	T	F	S
				1	2	3
4	5	6	7	8	9	10
11	12	13	14	15	16	17
18	19	20	21	22	23	24
25	26	27	28	29	30	31

AUGUST

S	M	T	W	T	F	S
1	2	3	4	5	6	7
8	9	10	11	12	13	14
15	16	17	18	19	20	21
22	23	24	25	26	27	28
29	30	31				

17
saturday

Full Moon ○

18
sunday

July

19
monday

20
tuesday

21
wednesday

22
thursday

23
friday

24
saturday

25
sunday

Mahavatar Babaji Commemoration Day

JULY

S	M	T	W	T	F	S
				1	2	3
4	5	6	7	8	9	10
11	12	13	14	15	16	17
18	19	20	21	22	23	24
25	26	27	28	29	30	31

AUGUST

S	M	T	W	T	F	S
1	2	3	4	5	6	7
8	9	10	11	12	13	14
15	16	17	18	19	20	21
22	23	24	25	26	27	28
29	30	31				

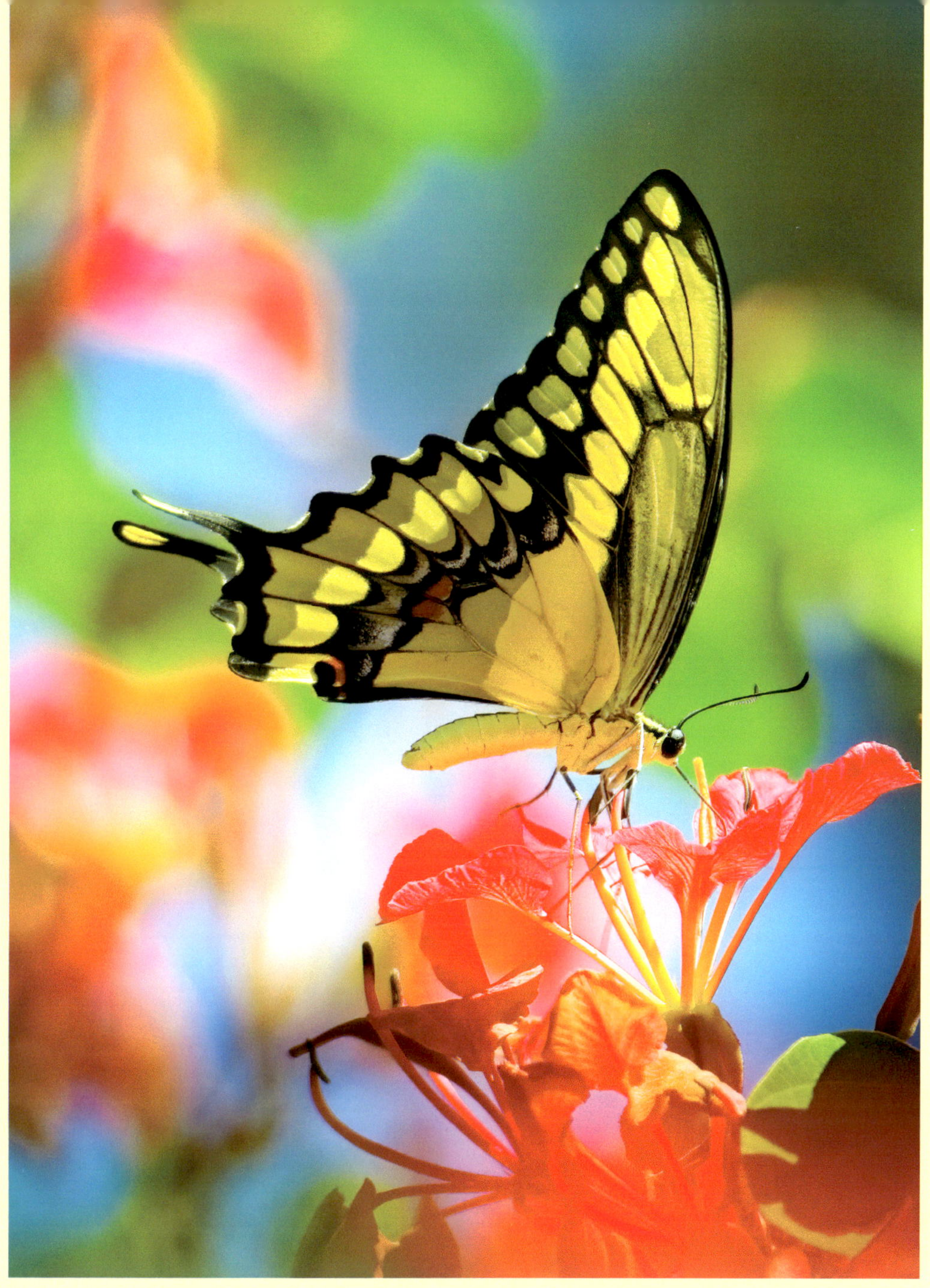

In each soul is the unique imprint of the grace of God.
Nowhere in the world is there another exactly like you.

—Paramahansa Yogananda

Giant Swallowtail Butterfly, San Diego, California   Photograph by Tom & Pat Leeson

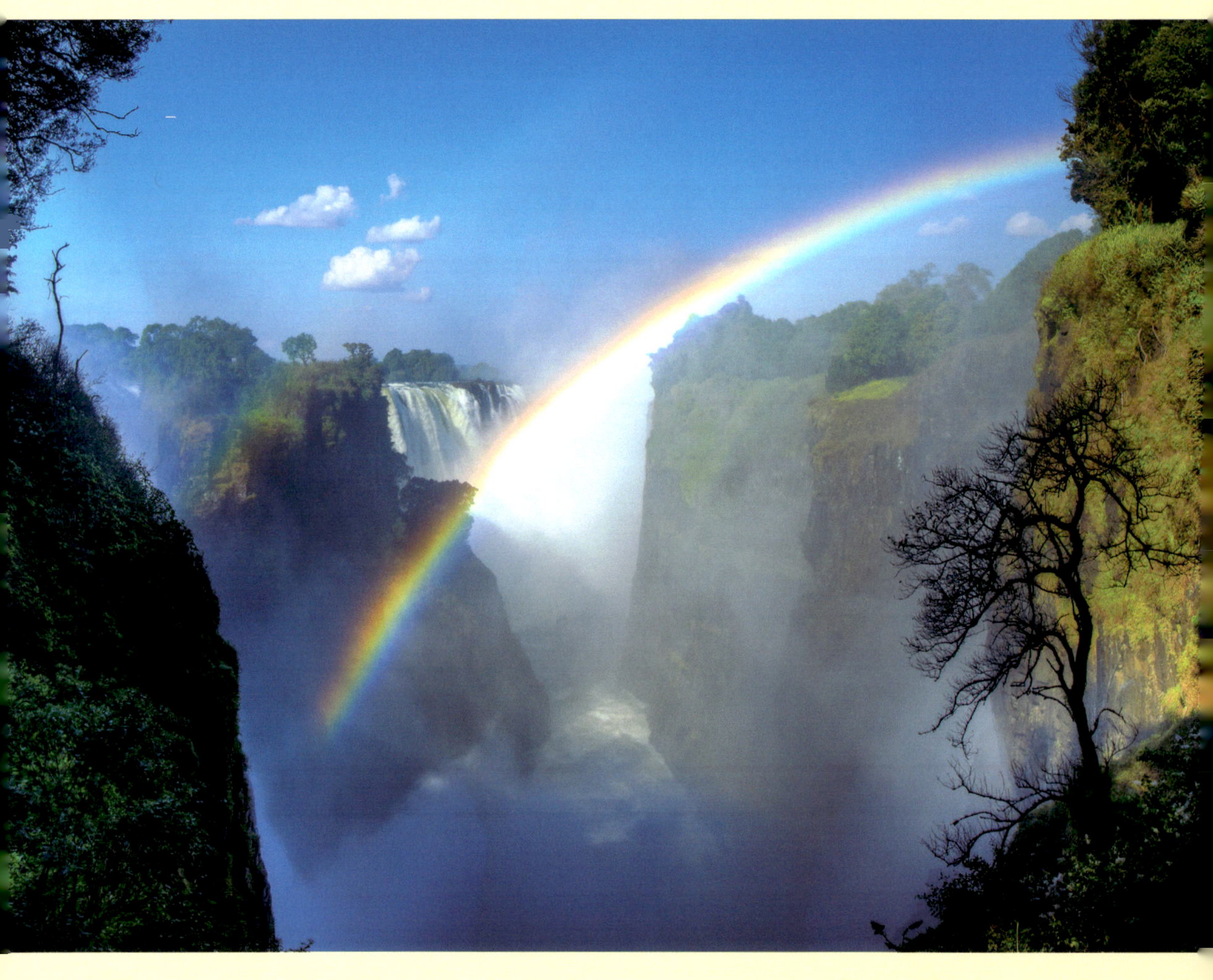

Meditation forms the rainbow bridge by which you can reach God.

—Paramahansa Yogananda

Victoria Falls, Zimbabwe Photograph by Burt Jones/Maurine Shimlock

July/August

Last Quarter ◑

26
monday

27
tuesday

28
wednesday

29
thursday

30
friday

JULY

S	M	T	W	T	F	S
				1	2	3
4	5	6	7	8	9	10
11	12	13	14	15	16	17
18	19	20	21	22	23	24
25	26	27	28	29	30	31

31
saturday

AUGUST

S	M	T	W	T	F	S
1	2	3	4	5	6	7
8	9	10	11	12	13	14
15	16	17	18	19	20	21
22	23	24	25	26	27	28
29	30	31				

1
sunday

August

2
monday

New Moon ●

3
tuesday

4
wednesday

5
thursday

6
friday

7
saturday

8
sunday

First Quarter ◐

AUGUST

S	M	T	W	T	F	S
1	2	3	4	5	6	7
8	9	10	11	12	13	14
15	16	17	18	19	20	21
22	23	24	25	26	27	28
29	30	31				

SEPTEMBER

S	M	T	W	T	F	S
			1	2	3	4
5	6	7	8	9	10	11
12	13	14	15	16	17	18
19	20	21	22	23	24	25
26	27	28	29	30		

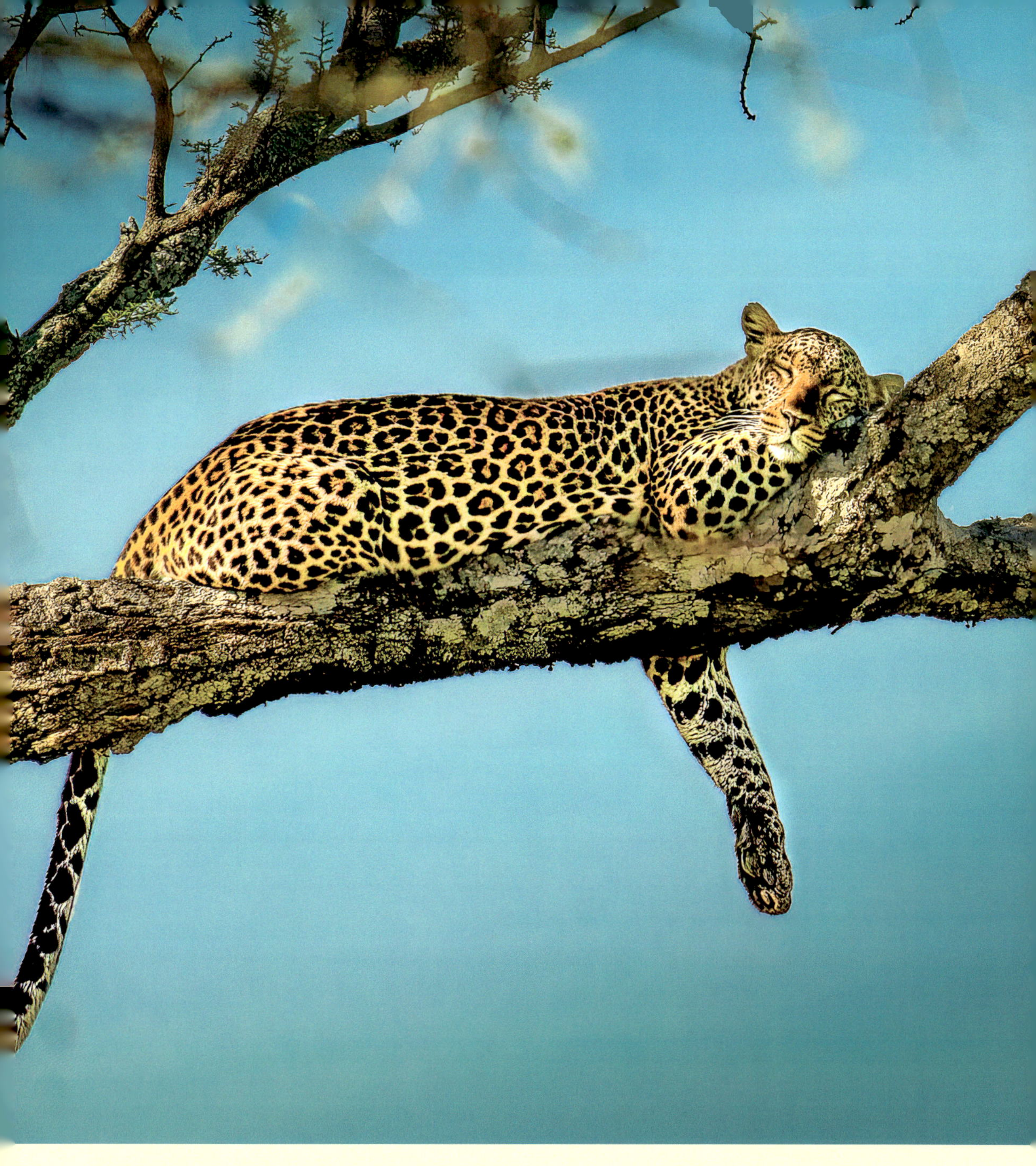

Just relax mentally and surrender yourself to the infinite silence,
forgetting time and all extraneous thoughts,
and you will begin to experience the wonders of divine consciousness.

—Paramahansa Yogananda

Sleeping leopard, Serengeti National Park, Tanzania   Photograph by Boyd Norton

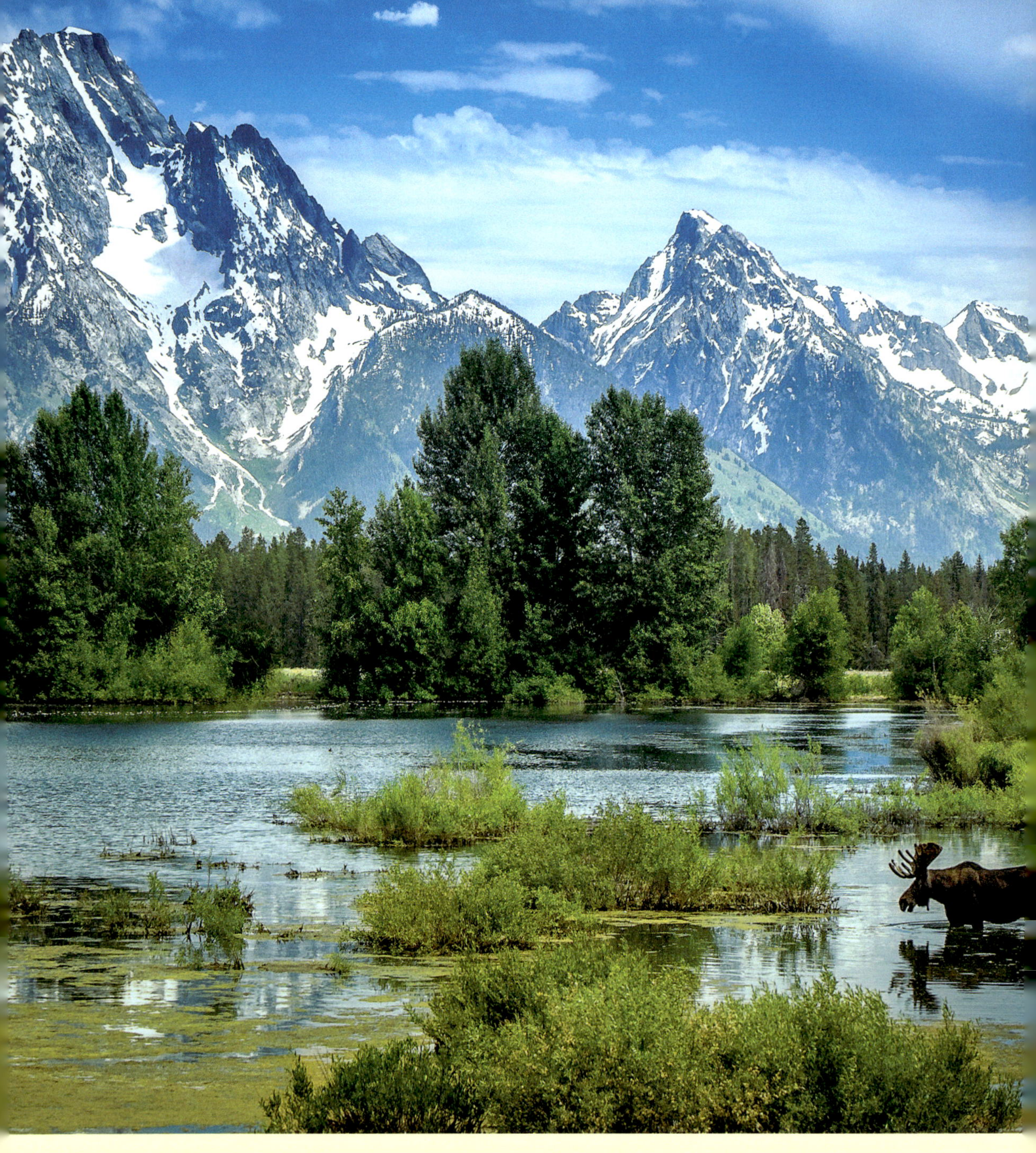

Spirit is the ultimate Reality....When you connect with that Power, all your desires become fulfilled; all your thirst for knowledge becomes quenched; all your hunger for truth becomes satisfied.

—Paramahansa Yogananda

Bull moose, Grand Teton National Park, Wyoming Photograph by Jim Stamates/Minden Pictures

August

9
monday

10
tuesday

11
wednesday

12
thursday

13
friday

AUGUST

S	M	T	W	T	F	S
1	2	3	4	5	6	7
8	9	10	11	12	13	14
15	16	17	18	19	20	21
22	23	24	25	26	27	28
29	30	31				

SEPTEMBER

S	M	T	W	T	F	S
			1	2	3	4
5	6	7	8	9	10	11
12	13	14	15	16	17	18
19	20	21	22	23	24	25
26	27	28	29	30		

14
saturday

15
sunday

August

16
monday

17
tuesday

Full Moon ○

18
wednesday

19
thursday

20
friday

21
saturday

22
sunday

AUGUST

S	M	T	W	T	F	S
1	2	3	4	5	6	7
8	9	10	11	12	13	14
15	16	17	18	19	20	21
22	23	24	25	26	27	28
29	30	31				

SEPTEMBER

S	M	T	W	T	F	S
			1	2	3	4
5	6	7	8	9	10	11
12	13	14	15	16	17	18
19	20	21	22	23	24	25
26	27	28	29	30		

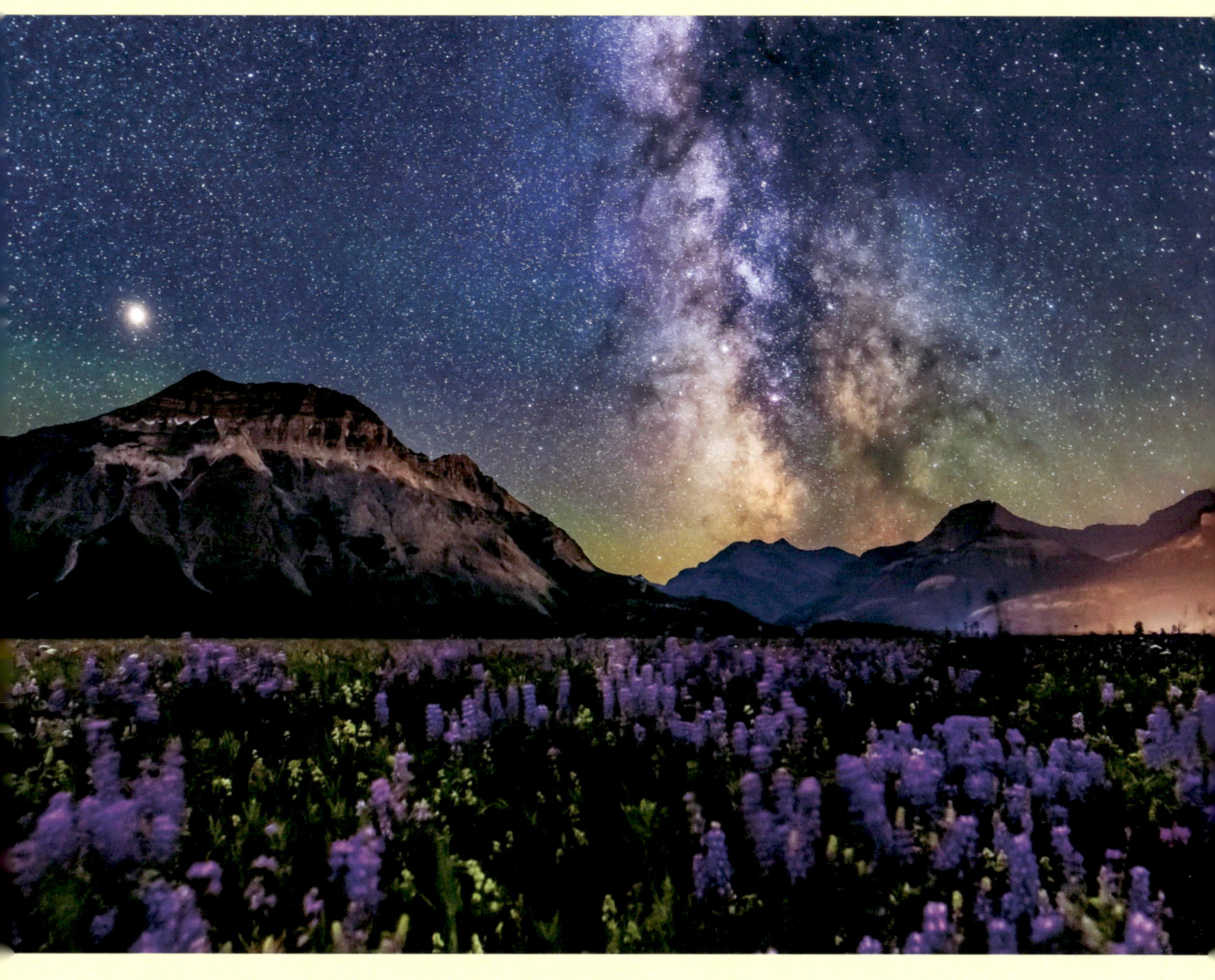

You are a part of the Eternal Life. Awaken and expand
your consciousness in God
so that your concept of yourself ceases to be limited to the little body.

—Paramahansa Yogananda

Milky Way, Waterton Lakes National Park, Alberta, Canada Photograph by Alan Dyer/AKM Images

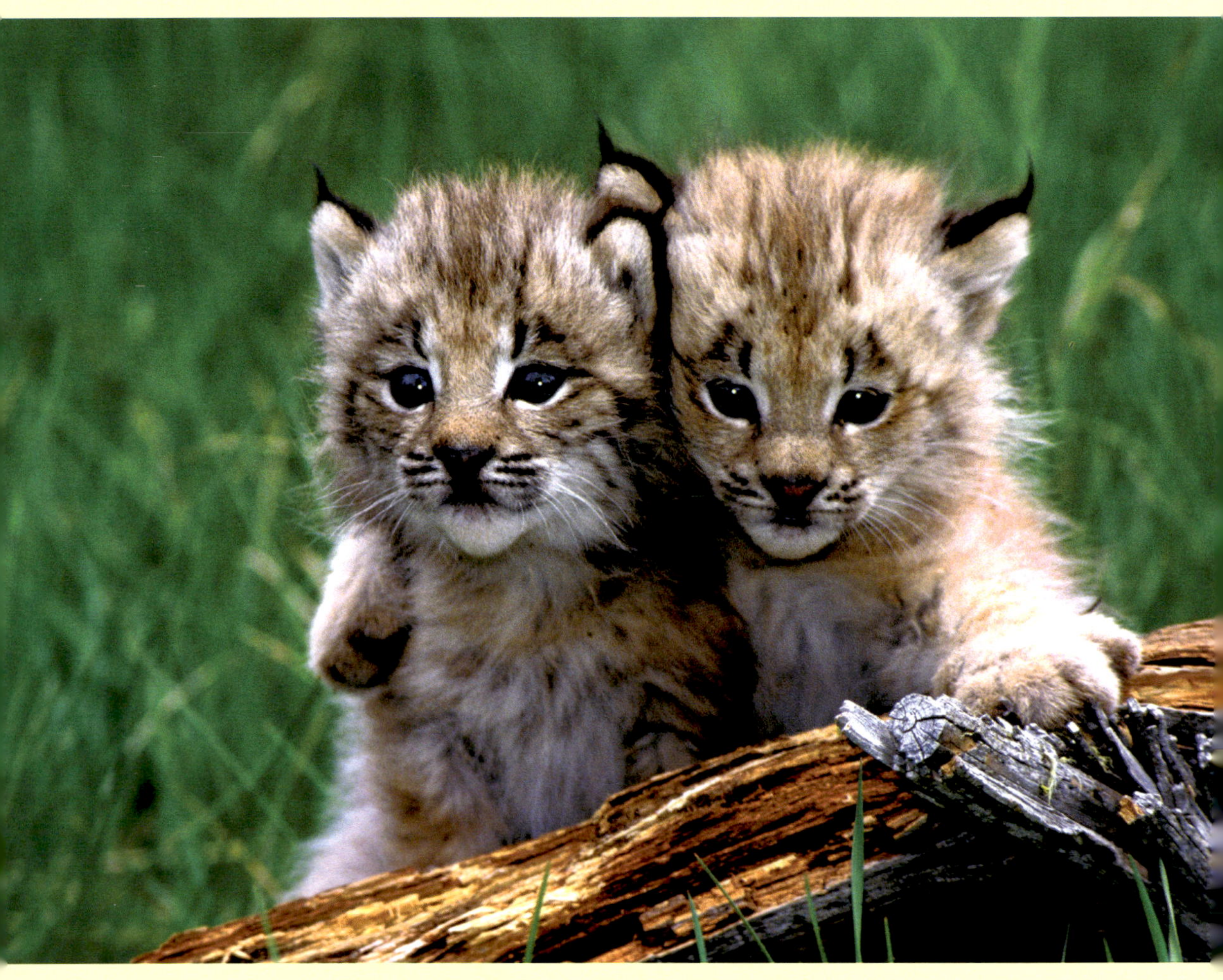

True friendship unites two souls so completely
that they reflect the unity of Spirit and its divine qualities.

—Paramahansa Yogananda

Lynx kittens, Rocky Mountains National Park, Colorado Photograph by Robert Barber/AKM Images

August

23
monday

Last Quarter ◑

24
tuesday

Janmashtami

25
wednesday

26
thursday

27
friday

August

S	M	T	W	T	F	S
1	2	3	4	5	6	7
8	9	10	11	12	13	14
15	16	17	18	19	20	21
22	23	24	25	26	27	28
29	30	31				

28
saturday

September

S	M	T	W	T	F	S
			1	2	3	4
5	6	7	8	9	10	11
12	13	14	15	16	17	18
19	20	21	22	23	24	25
26	27	28	29	30		

29
sunday

August/September

30
monday

31
tuesday

New Moon ●

1
wednesday

2
thursday

3
friday

4
saturday

5
sunday

AUGUST

S	M	T	W	T	F	S
1	2	3	4	5	6	7
8	9	10	11	12	13	14
15	16	17	18	19	20	21
22	23	24	25	26	27	28
29	30	31				

SEPTEMBER

S	M	T	W	T	F	S
			1	2	3	4
5	6	7	8	9	10	11
12	13	14	15	16	17	18
19	20	21	22	23	24	25
26	27	28	29	30		

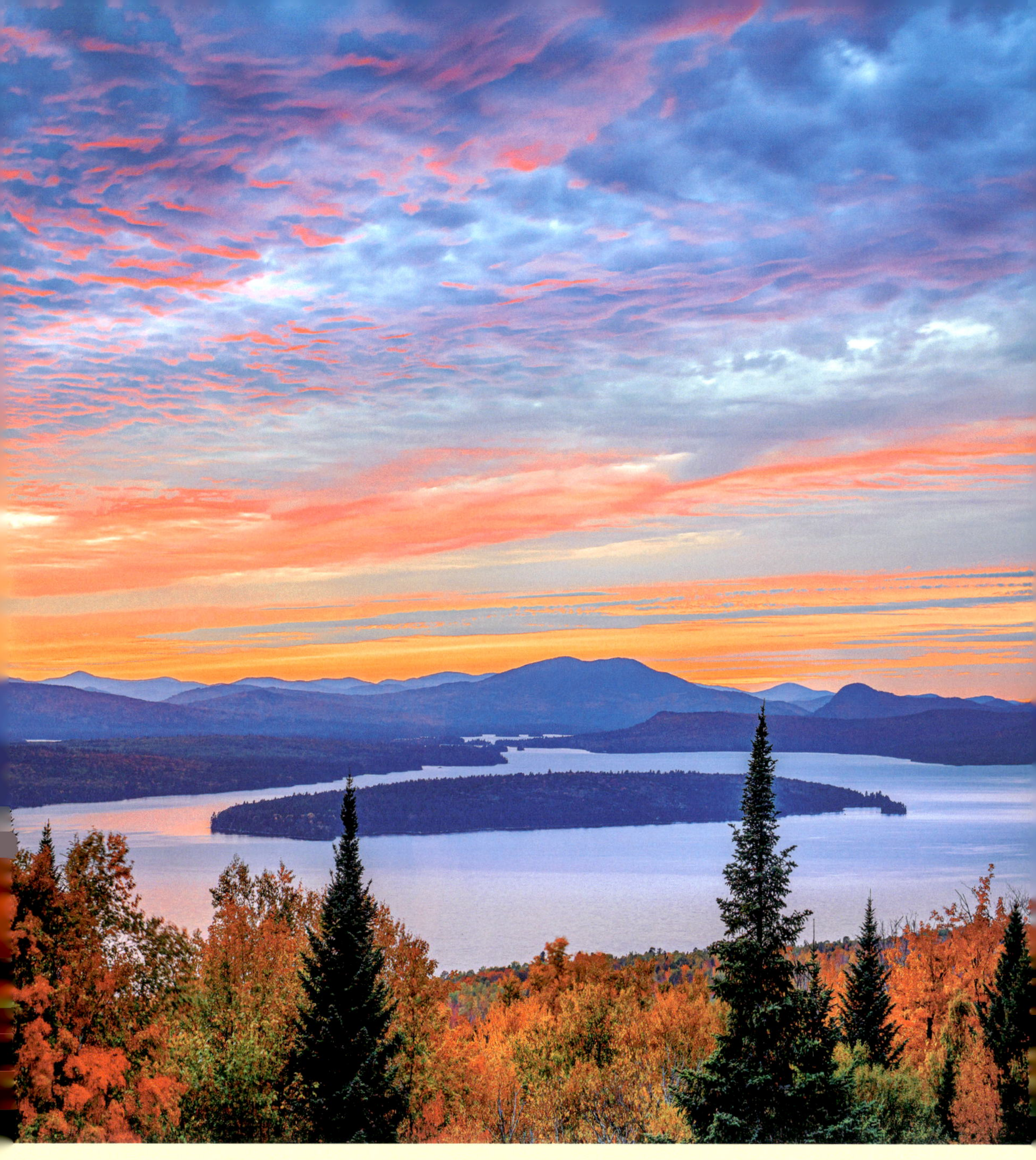

Learn to be still in body and mind, for where motion ceases, there begins the perception of God.

—Paramahansa Yogananda

Mooselookmeguntic Lake, Franklin County, Maine   Photograph by Paul Rezendes

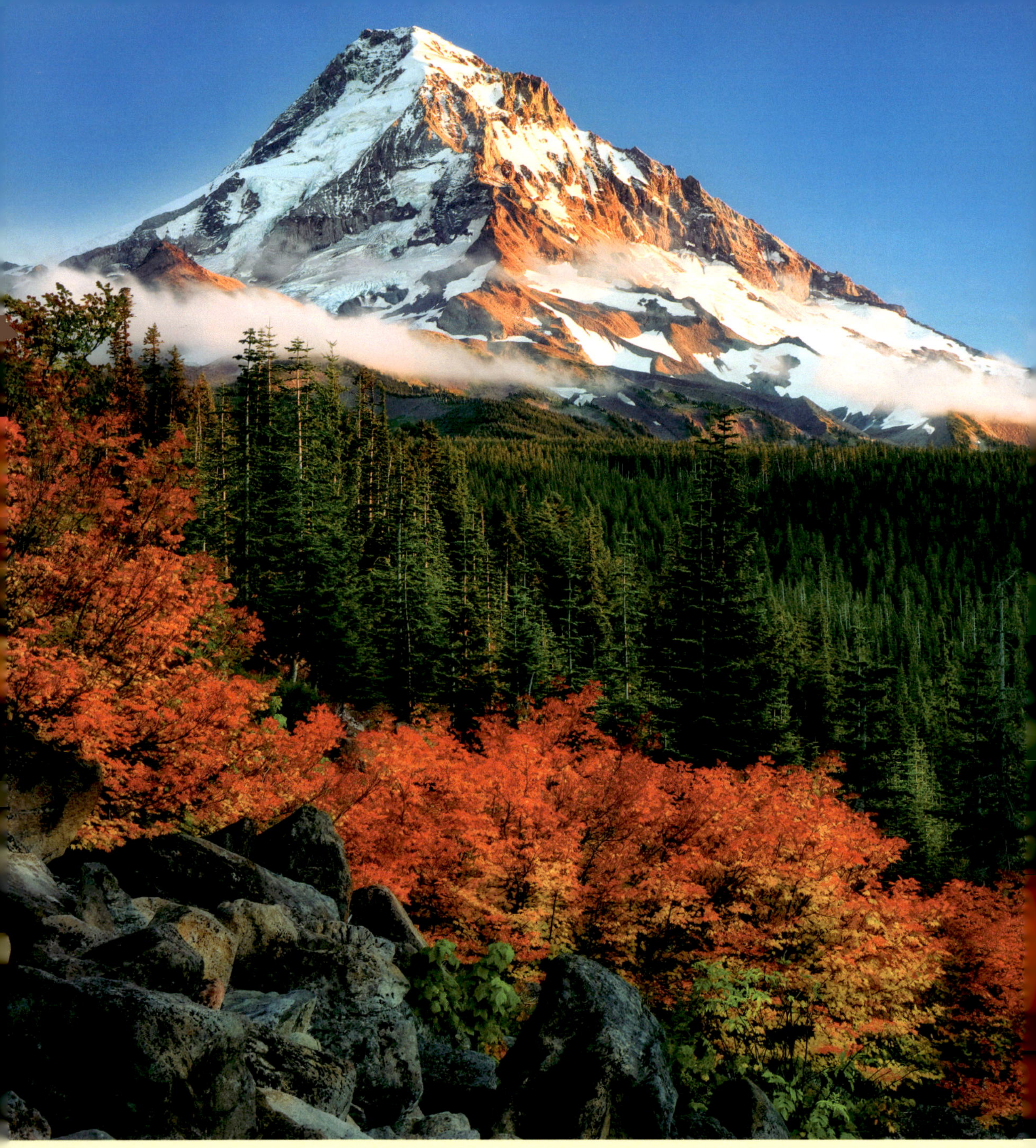

*W*ill is a tremendous factor in life.
It is the power by which you can reach the heights of God-realization.

—Paramahansa Yogananda

Mount Hood from Vista Ridge, Oregon   Photograph by Larry Geddis

September

Labor Day (U.S. and Canada)

6 monday

First Quarter ◐

7 tuesday

8 wednesday

9 thursday

10 friday

SEPTEMBER

S	M	T	W	T	F	S
			1	2	3	4
5	6	7	8	9	10	11
12	13	14	15	16	17	18
19	20	21	22	23	24	25
26	27	28	29	30		

11 saturday

OCTOBER

S	M	T	W	T	F	S
					1	2
3	4	5	6	7	8	9
10	11	12	13	14	15	16
17	18	19	20	21	22	23
24/31	25	26	27	28	29	30

12 sunday

September

13
monday

14
tuesday

15
wednesday

Full Moon ○

16
thursday

17
friday

18
saturday

19
sunday

SEPTEMBER

S	M	T	W	T	F	S
			1	2	3	4
5	6	7	8	9	10	11
12	13	14	15	16	17	18
19	20	21	22	23	24	25
26	27	28	29	30		

OCTOBER

S	M	T	W	T	F	S
					1	2
3	4	5	6	7	8	9
10	11	12	13	14	15	16
17	18	19	20	21	22	23
24/31	25	26	27	28	29	30

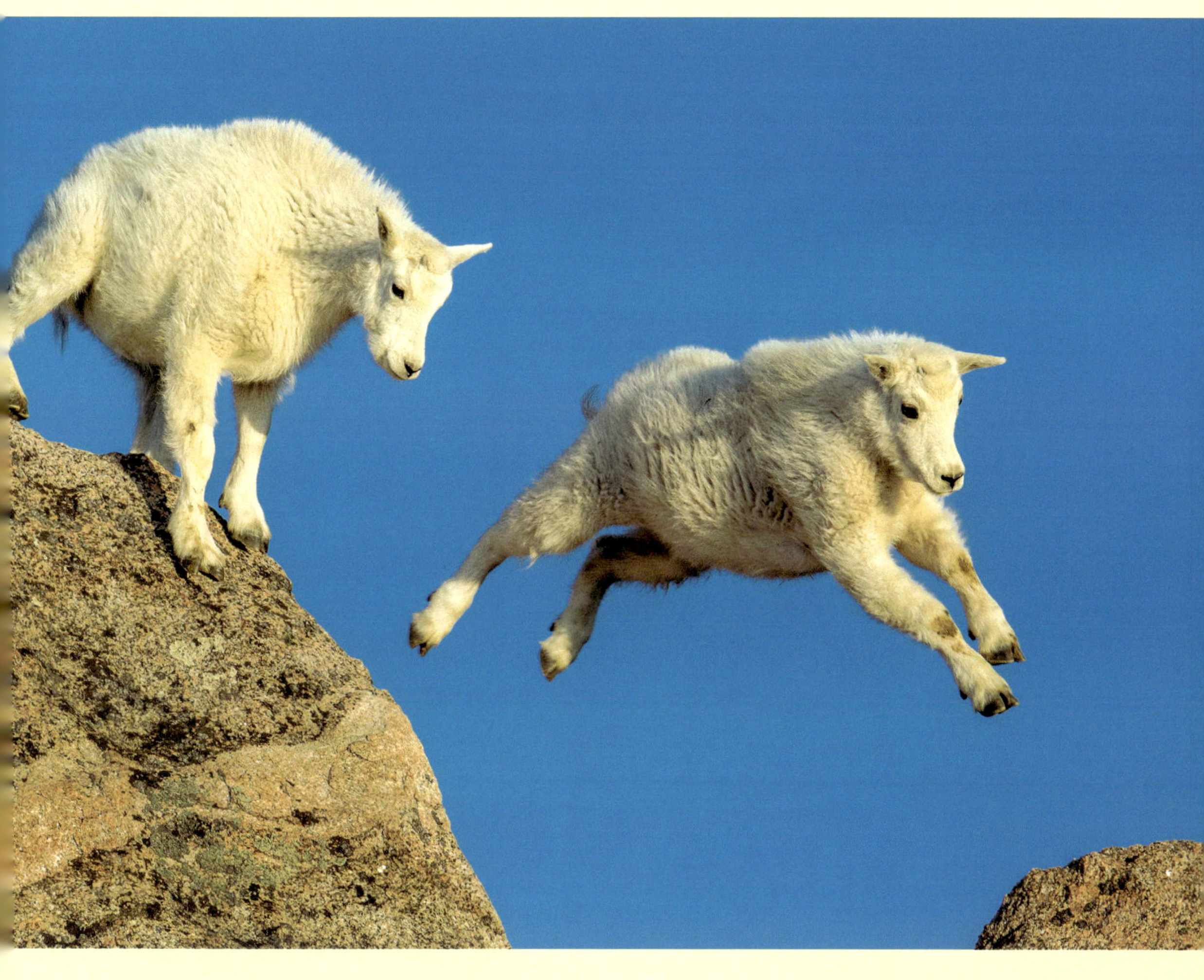

We must be fearless, sincere, surrounded not only with those whom we can inspire, but with those who can inspire us as well.

—Paramahansa Yogananda

Mountain Goat kids, Mount Evans Wilderness, Colorado   Photograph by Russ Burden

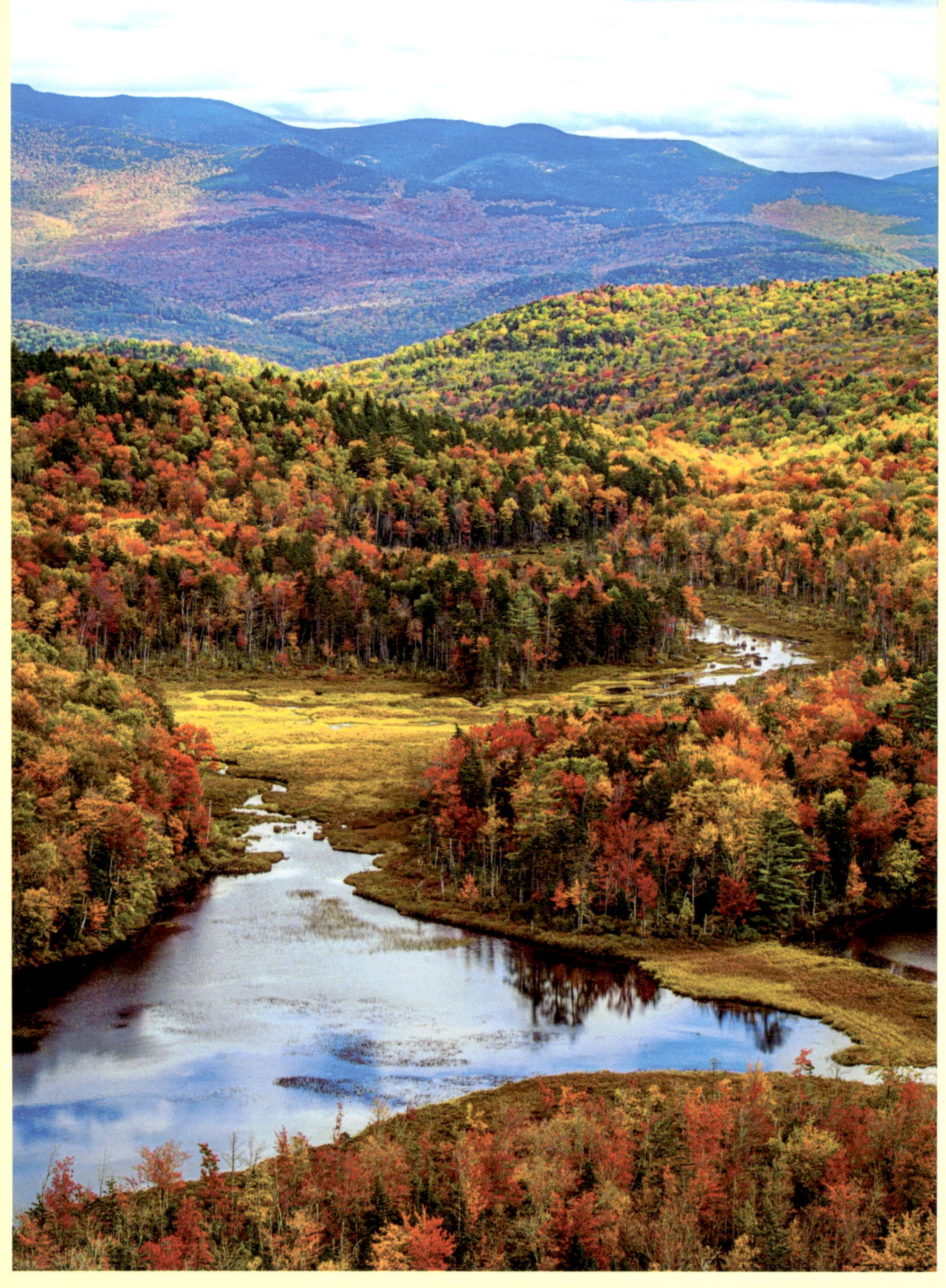

Feel the hidden waters of Spirit trickling through all material life;
and during all your activities secretly imbibe
from that sacred wellspring in your soul.

—Paramahansa Yogananda

Appalachian Mountains and Elbow Pond, New Hampshire Photograph by Paul Rezendes

September

20
monday

UN International Day of Peace

21
tuesday

Autumnal Equinox

22
wednesday

Last Quarter ◑

23
thursday

24
friday

SEPTEMBER

S	M	T	W	T	F	S
			1	2	3	4
5	6	7	8	9	10	11
12	13	14	15	16	17	18
19	20	21	22	23	24	25
26	27	28	29	30		

25
saturday

OCTOBER

S	M	T	W	T	F	S
					1	2
3	4	5	6	7	8	9
10	11	12	13	14	15	16
17	18	19	20	21	22	23
24/31	25	26	27	28	29	30

Lahiri Mahasaya's Mahasamadhi

26
sunday

September/October

27
monday

28
tuesday

29
wednesday
New Moon ●

30
thursday
Lahiri Mahasaya's Birthday

1
friday
Rosh Hashanah

2
saturday

3
sunday

September

S	M	T	W	T	F	S
			1	2	3	4
5	6	7	8	9	10	11
12	13	14	15	16	17	18
19	20	21	22	23	24	25
26	27	28	29	30		

October

S	M	T	W	T	F	S
					1	2
3	4	5	6	7	8	9
10	11	12	13	14	15	16
17	18	19	20	21	22	23
24/31	25	26	27	28	29	30

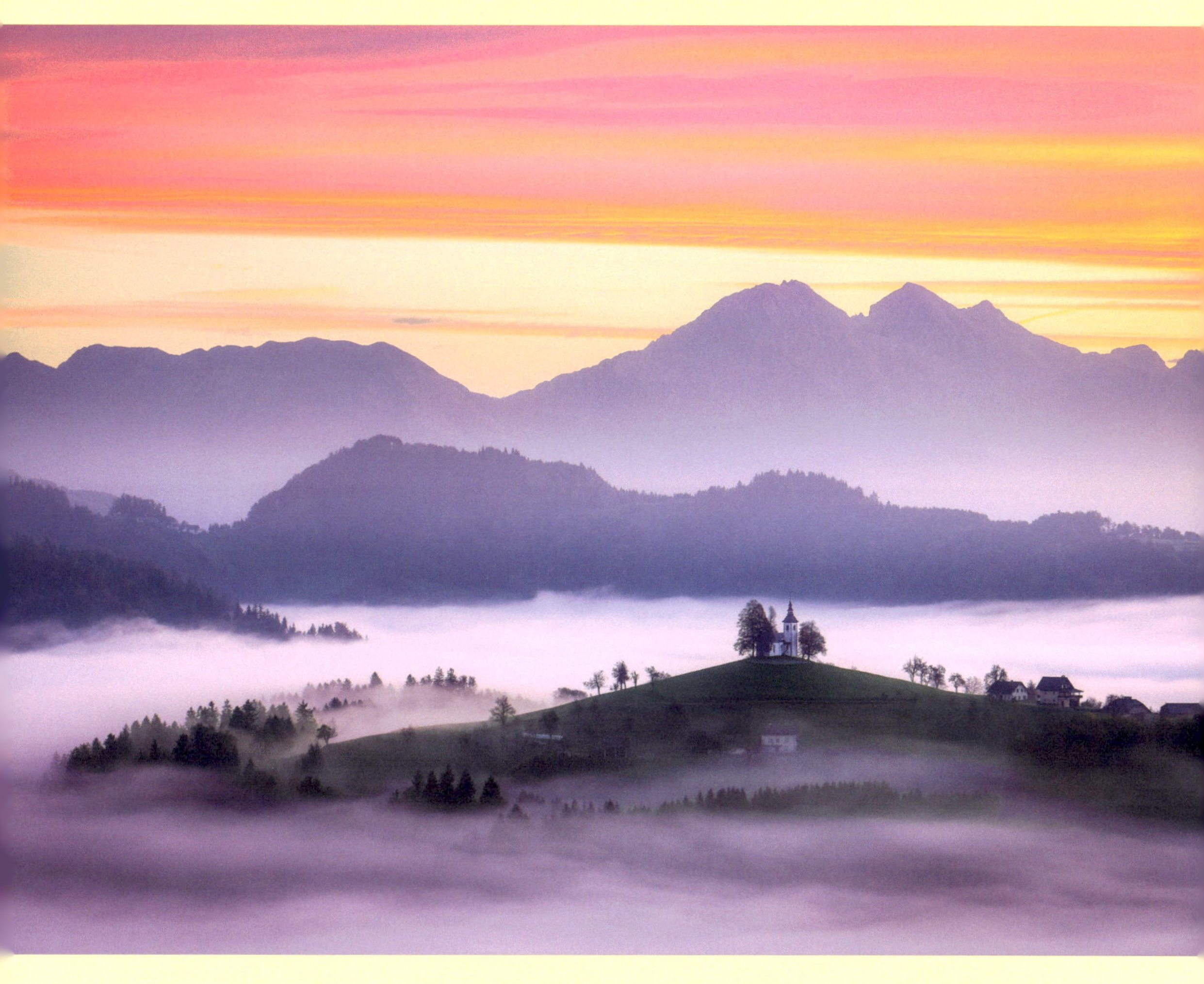

I am in the temple of quietness. Thine eternal kingdom of peace is spread tier upon tier before my gaze.

—Paramahansa Yogananda

Sveti Tomaž, Slovenia   Photograph by Guy Edwardes

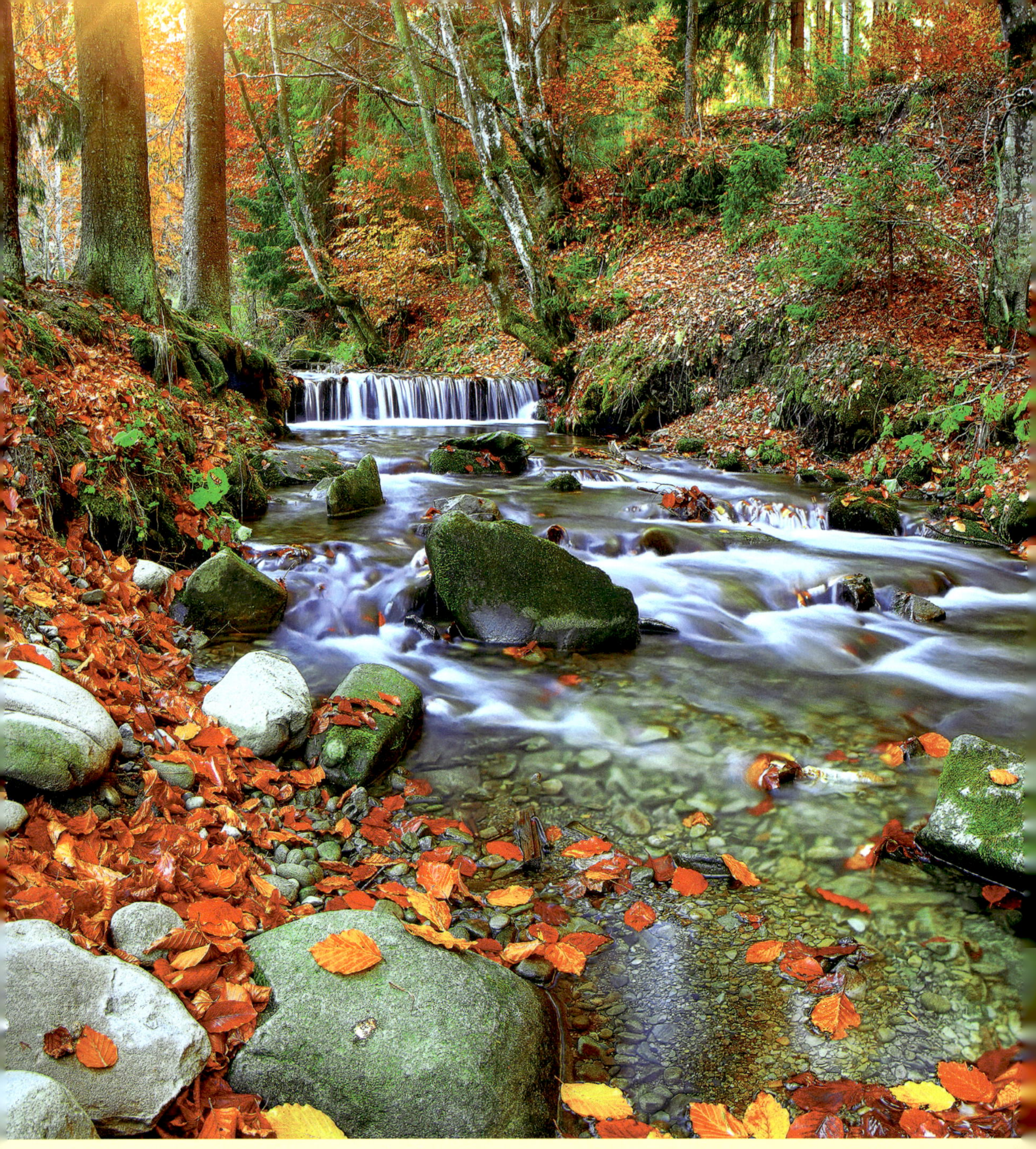

Be inwardly ever newly joyous, like the ever-fresh laughing waters of a gurgling brook.

—Paramahansa Yogananda

Carpathian Mountains, Slovakia   Photograph by Vadym Lavra

October

4
monday

5
tuesday

6
wednesday

First Quarter ◐

7
thursday

8
friday

OCTOBER

S	M	T	W	T	F	S
					1	2
3	4	5	6	7	8	9
10	11	12	13	14	15	16
17	18	19	20	21	22	23
24/31	25	26	27	28	29	30

NOVEMBER

S	M	T	W	T	F	S
	1	2	3	4	5	6
7	8	9	10	11	12	13
14	15	16	17	18	19	20
21	22	23	24	25	26	27
28	29	30				

9
saturday

Yom Kippur

10
sunday

October

11
monday

Columbus Day/Indigenous Peoples' Day   Thanksgiving Day (Canada)

12
tuesday

13
wednesday

14
thursday

15
friday

Full Moon ○

16
saturday

17
sunday

October

S	M	T	W	T	F	S
					1	2
3	4	5	6	7	8	9
10	11	12	13	14	15	16
17	18	19	20	21	22	23
24/31	25	26	27	28	29	30

November

S	M	T	W	T	F	S
	1	2	3	4	5	6
7	8	9	10	11	12	13
14	15	16	17	18	19	20
21	22	23	24	25	26	27
28	29	30				

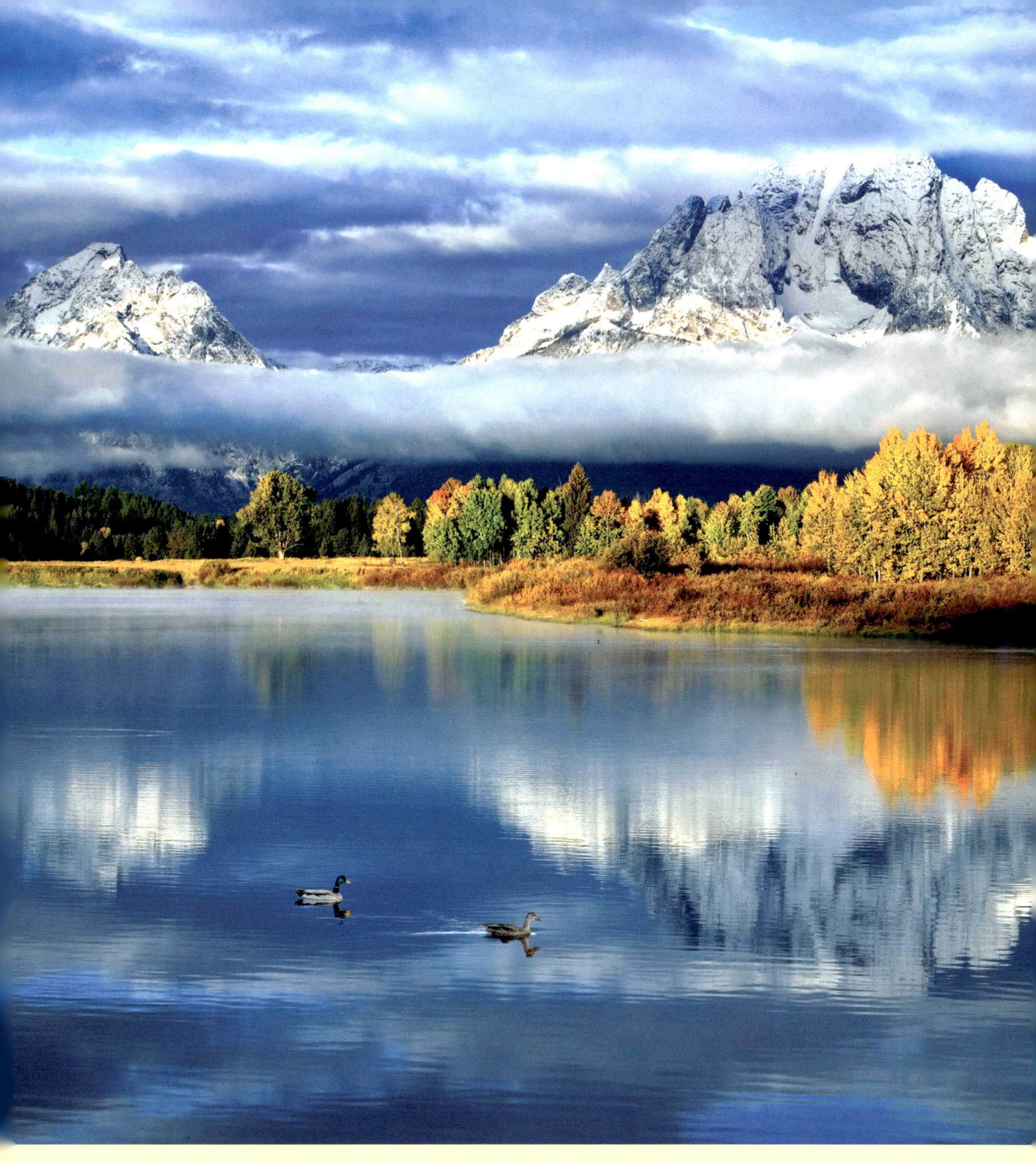

There is a living relationship, a living communion, linking all animate and inanimate creatures in this world—an immanent intelligence which is trying to bring out the God-essence that is everywhere veiled.

—Paramahansa Yogananda

Snake River, Grand Teton National Park, Wyoming   Photograph by Dennis Frates

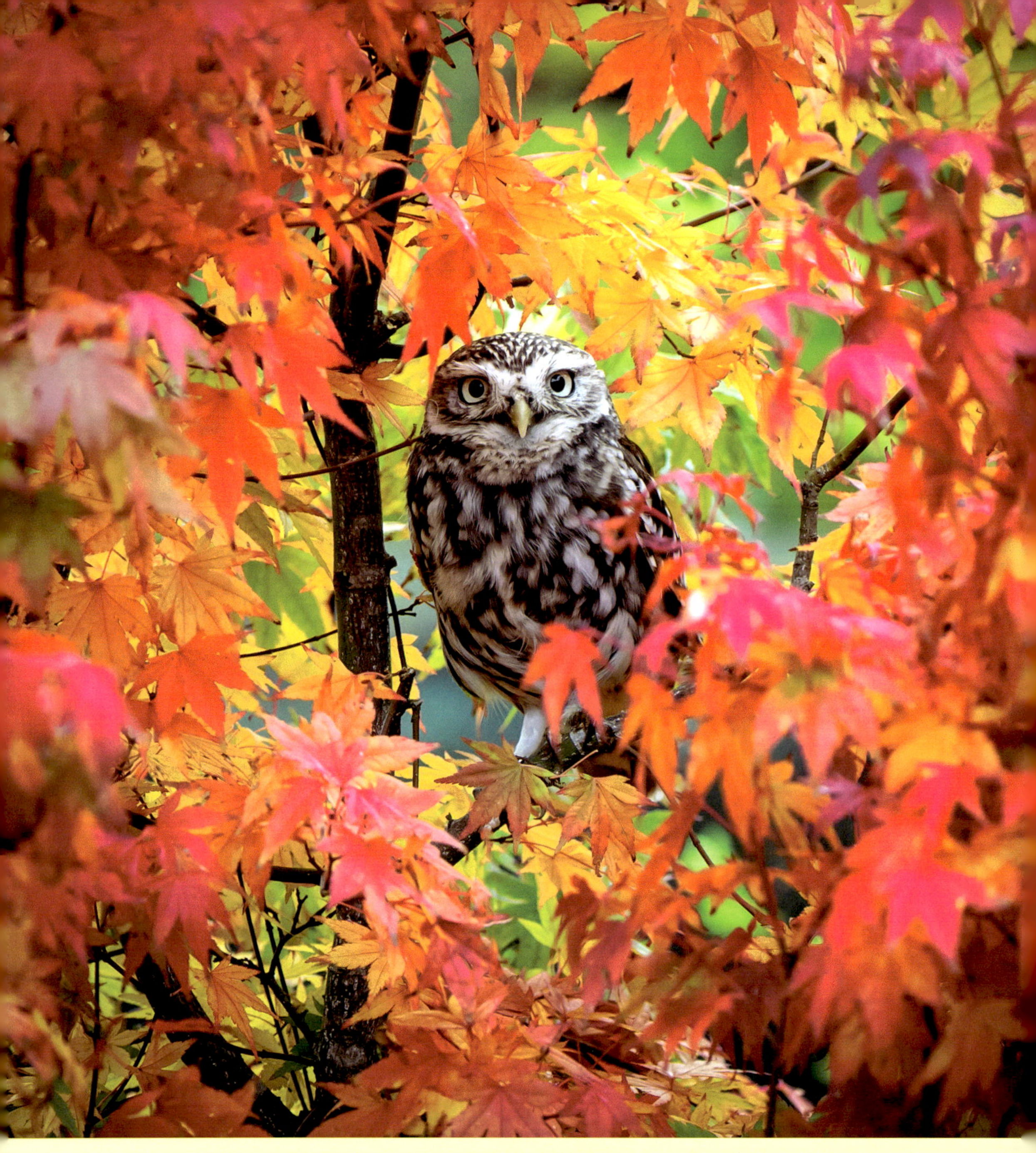

When you are calm and at peace within,
you love everyone and feel friendly toward all.
This is the harmony God intended for His creation.

—Paramahansa Yogananda

Little Owl in Japanese Maple tree, England Photograph by Frederick Desmette/SUPERSTOCK

Your

2028 INNER REFLECTIONS ENGAGEMENT CALENDAR

is now available online and in select bookstores

You may also place your order directly from Self-Realization Fellowship by calling 818-549-5151 Monday – Friday from 9:00 a.m. to 5:00 p.m. Pacific time or order online at:
srfbooks.org

If you would like to receive inspiring wisdom from Paramahansa Yogananda and regular updates on news and events from Self-Realization Fellowship, please sign up for our Newsletter at:
yogananda.org/subscribe

If you would like a free copy of Self-Realization Fellowship's complete catalog of books and recordings, please call the number above or fill out the form below and mail to:

Self-Realization Fellowship
3880 San Rafael Ave.
Los Angeles, CA 90065-3219 U.S.A.

Name: ____

Address: ______________________________________

City: ________________________ State: _____ Zip code: __________

Country: ______________________________________

October

18
monday

19
tuesday

20
wednesday

21
thursday

22
friday

Last Quarter ◑

23
saturday

24
sunday

October

S	M	T	W	T	F	S
					1	2
3	4	5	6	7	8	9
10	11	12	13	14	15	16
17	18	19	20	21	22	23
24/31	25	26	27	28	29	30

November

S	M	T	W	T	F	S
	1	2	3	4	5	6
7	8	9	10	11	12	13
14	15	16	17	18	19	20
21	22	23	24	25	26	27
28	29	30				

October

25
monday

26
tuesday

27
wednesday

28
thursday

29
friday

New Moon ●

30
saturday

31
sunday

Halloween (U.S., Canada, U.K.)
Daylight Saving Time ends (U.K. and European Union)

OCTOBER

S	M	T	W	T	F	S
					1	2
3	4	5	6	7	8	9
10	11	12	13	14	15	16
17	18	19	20	21	22	23
24/31	25	26	27	28	29	30

NOVEMBER

S	M	T	W	T	F	S
	1	2	3	4	5	6
7	8	9	10	11	12	13
14	15	16	17	18	19	20
21	22	23	24	25	26	27
28	29	30				

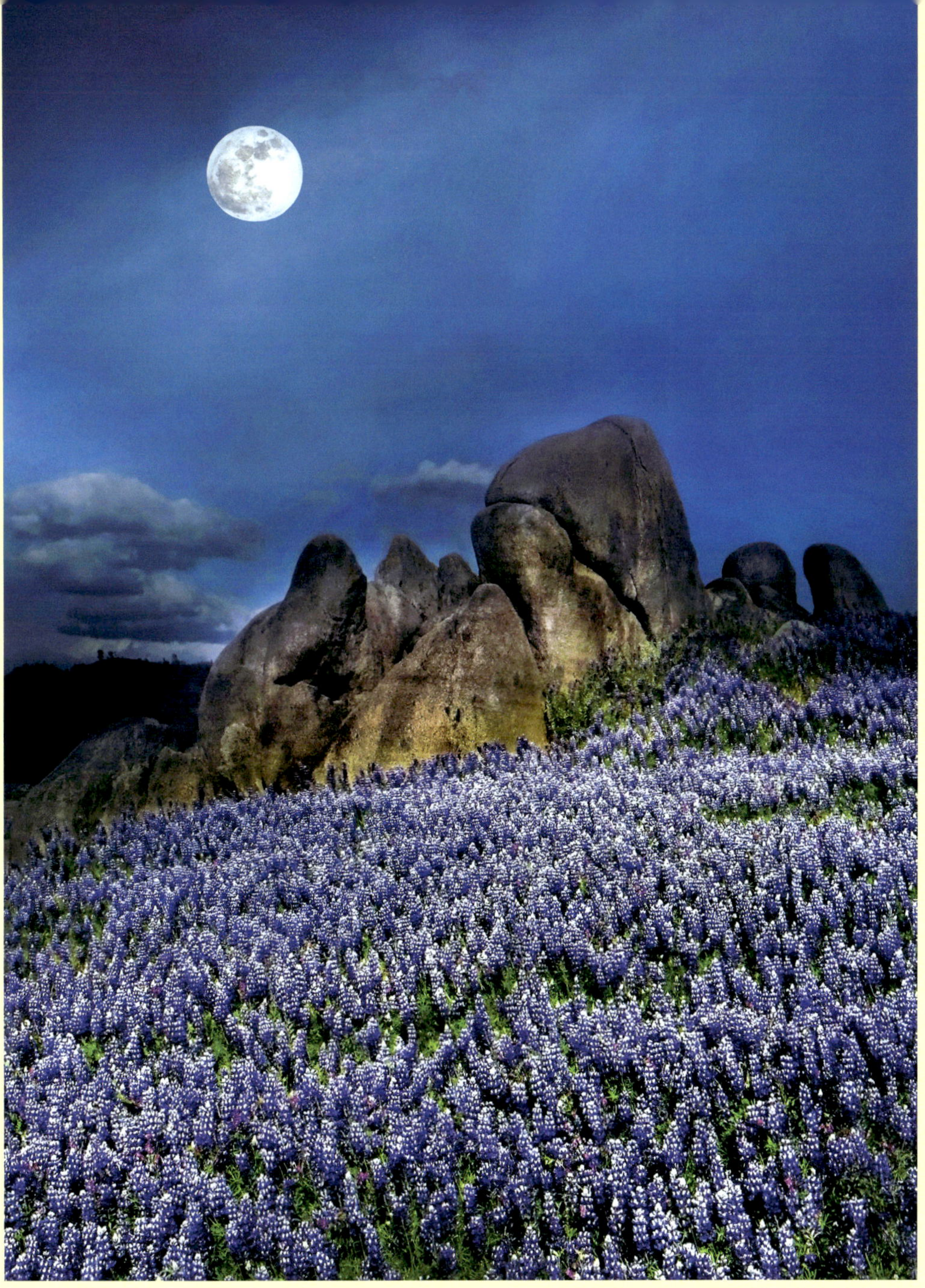

Once you have touched the Source of truth and life,
all nature will respond to you. Finding God within,
you will find Him without, in all people and all conditions.

—Paramahansa Yogananda

Supermoon over lupine field near Folsom Lake, California   Photograph by John Hendrickson

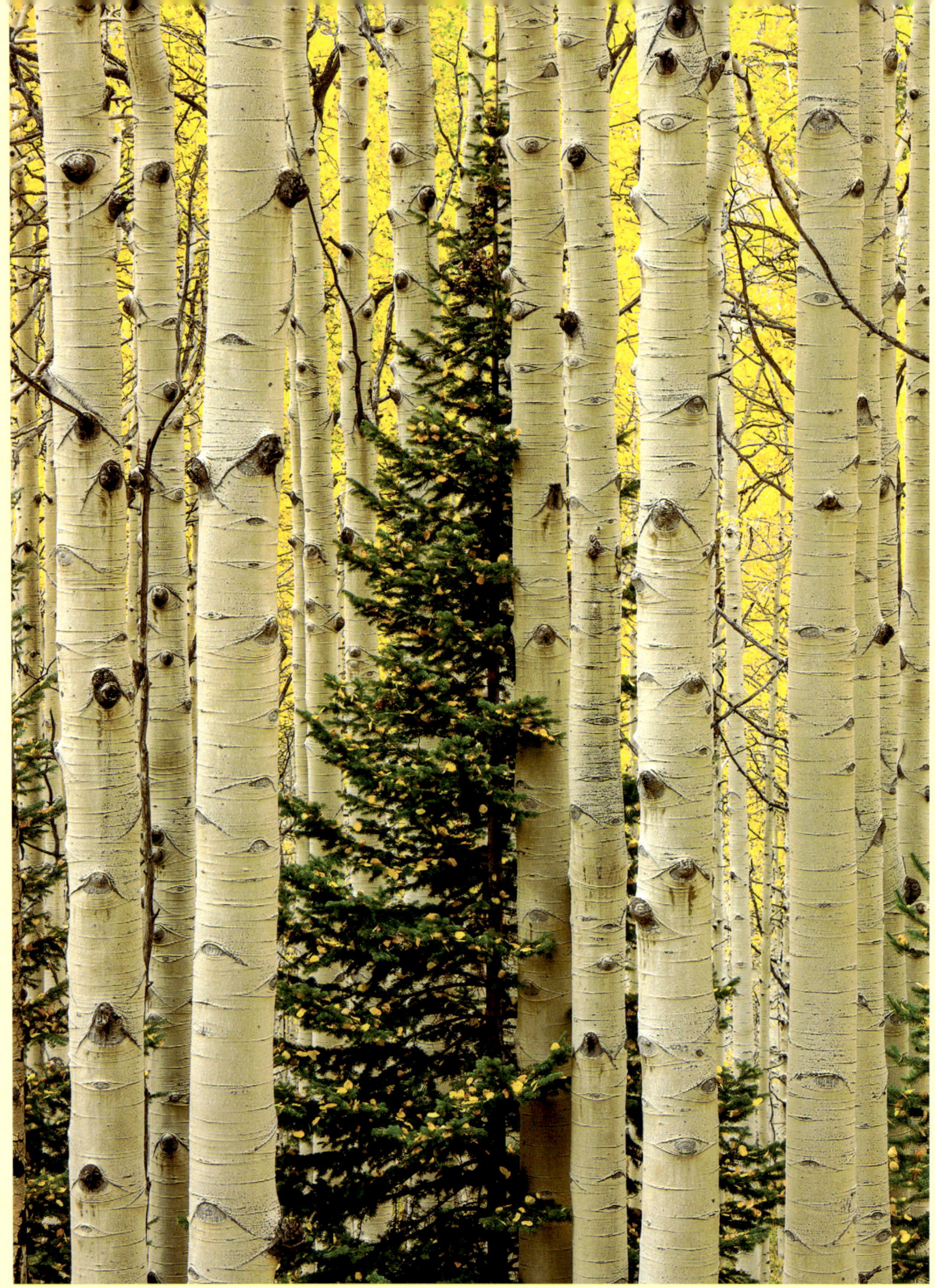

Love itself is never lost, but just plays hide-and-seek with you in many hearts; that in pursuing it you might find its ever greater manifestations.

—Paramahansa Yogananda

Aspen grove, Gunnison National Forest, Colorado   Photograph by Glenn Randall

November

1
monday

2
tuesday

3
wednesday

4
thursday

5
friday

NOVEMBER

S	M	T	W	T	F	S
	1	2	3	4	5	6
7	8	9	10	11	12	13
14	15	16	17	18	19	20
21	22	23	24	25	26	27
28	29	30				

First Quarter ◐

6
saturday

DECEMBER

S	M	T	W	T	F	S
			1	2	3	4
5	6	7	8	9	10	11
12	13	14	15	16	17	18
19	20	21	22	23	24	25
26	27	28	29	30	31	

Daylight Saving Time ends (U.S. and Canada)

7
sunday

November

8
monday

9
tuesday

10
wednesday

11
thursday
Veterans Day   Remembrance Day (Canada)

12
friday

13
saturday
Full Moon ○

14
sunday
Remembrance Sunday (U.K.)

NOVEMBER

S	M	T	W	T	F	S
	1	2	3	4	5	6
7	8	9	10	11	12	13
14	15	16	17	18	19	20
21	22	23	24	25	26	27
28	29	30				

DECEMBER

S	M	T	W	T	F	S
			1	2	3	4
5	6	7	8	9	10	11
12	13	14	15	16	17	18
19	20	21	22	23	24	25
26	27	28	29	30	31	

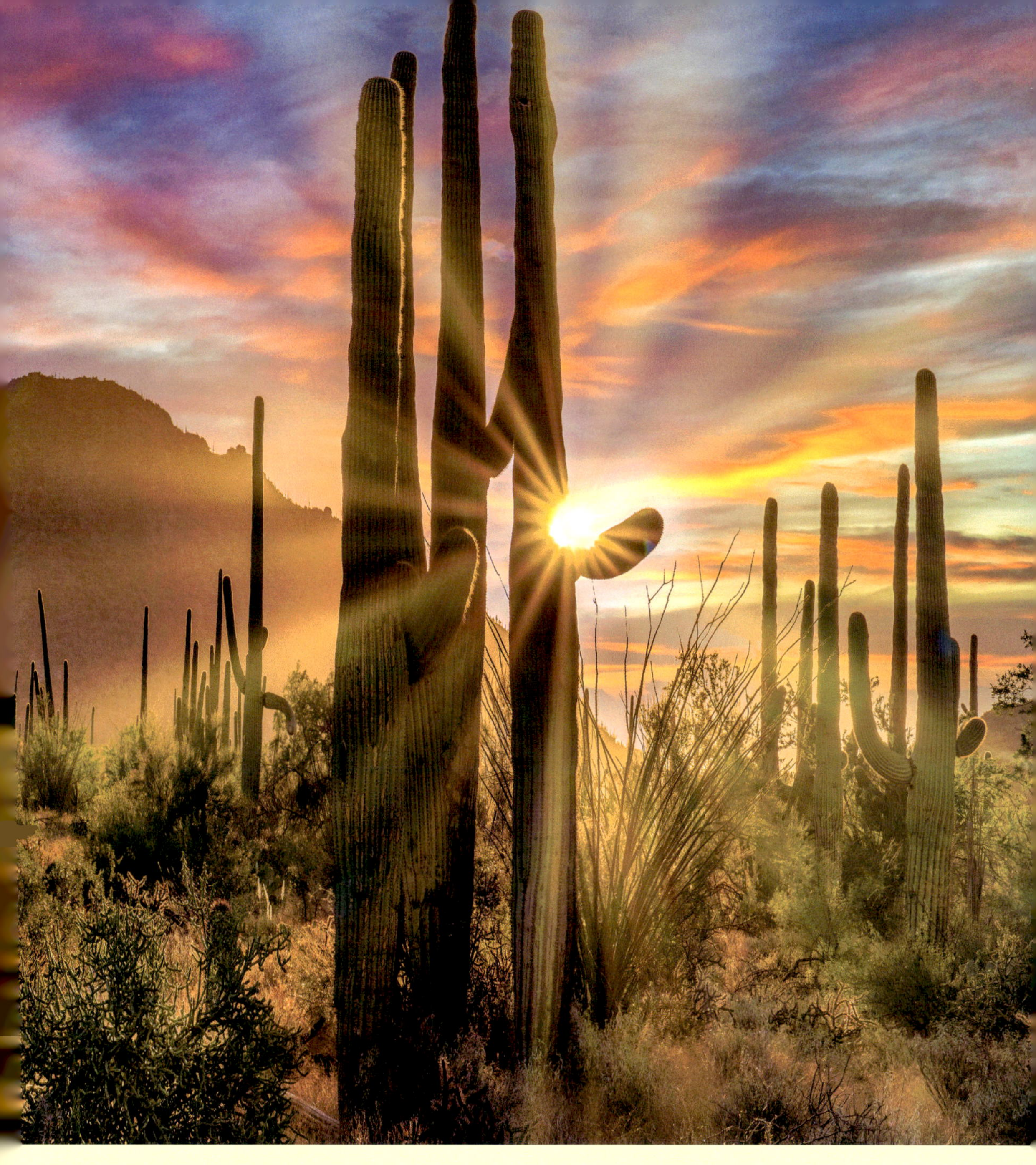

Your soul is a beacon of infinite power. You can expand that power from within and give light and health and understanding to others.

—Paramahansa Yogananda

Saguaro Cactus, Saguaro National Park West, Arizona   Photograph by Tim Fitzharris

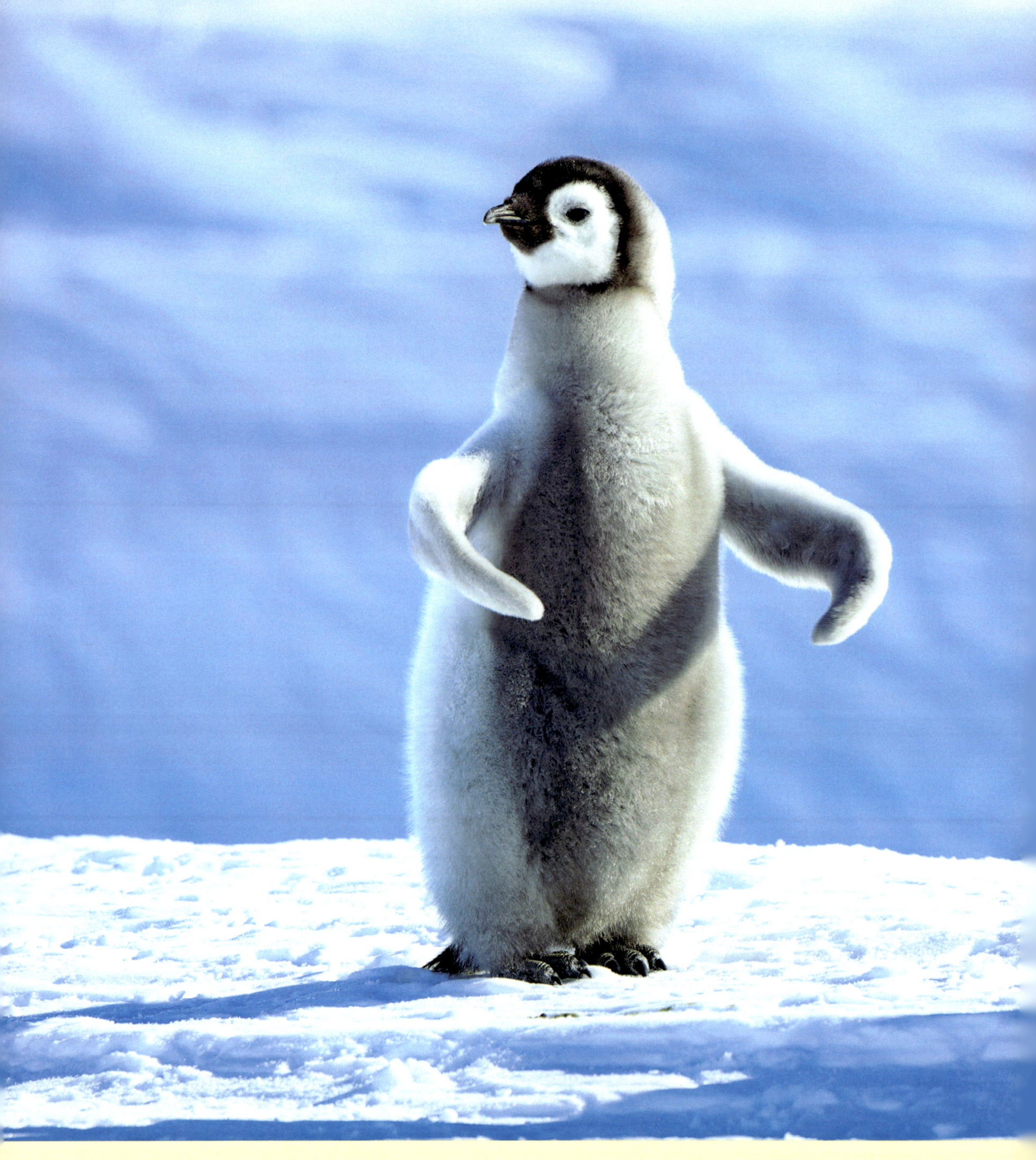

You are a child immortal. You have come on earth to entertain and to be entertained....
Awaken the innate fortitude of the mind by affirming,
"No matter what experiences come, they cannot touch me. I am always happy."

—Paramahansa Yogananda

Emperor Penguin chick, Gould Bay, Antarctica

Photograph by Roberta Olenick/Grandmaison Photography

November

15
monday

16
tuesday

17
wednesday

18
thursday

19
friday

20
saturday

Last Quarter ◑

21
sunday

NOVEMBER

S	M	T	W	T	F	S
	1	2	3	4	5	6
7	8	9	10	11	12	13
14	15	16	17	18	19	20
21	22	23	24	25	26	27
28	29	30				

DECEMBER

S	M	T	W	T	F	S
			1	2	3	4
5	6	7	8	9	10	11
12	13	14	15	16	17	18
19	20	21	22	23	24	25
26	27	28	29	30	31	

November

22
monday

23
tuesday

24
wednesday

25
thursday

Thanksgiving Day

26
friday

27
saturday

New Moon ●

28
sunday

NOVEMBER

S	M	T	W	T	F	S
	1	2	3	4	5	6
7	8	9	10	11	12	13
14	15	16	17	18	19	20
21	22	23	24	25	26	27
28	29	30				

DECEMBER

S	M	T	W	T	F	S
			1	2	3	4
5	6	7	8	9	10	11
12	13	14	15	16	17	18
19	20	21	22	23	24	25
26	27	28	29	30	31	

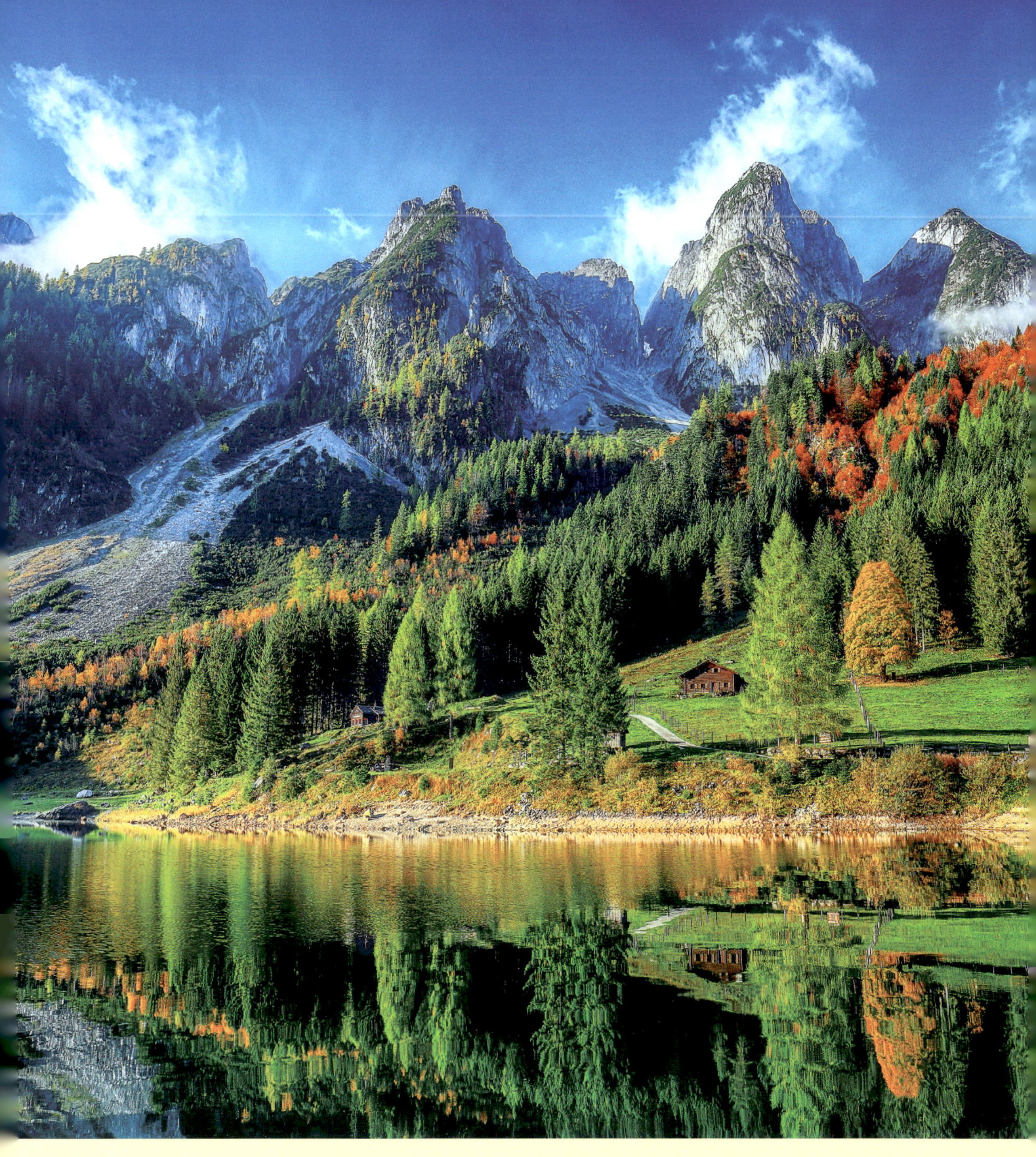

Our thoughts and words are the seeds that will bring forth
our harvest of the future. Therefore, I will begin today
to fill my consciousness with the ideas of abundance.

—Paramahansa Yogananda

Austrian Alps, near Salzburg, Austria   Photograph by Vadym Lavra

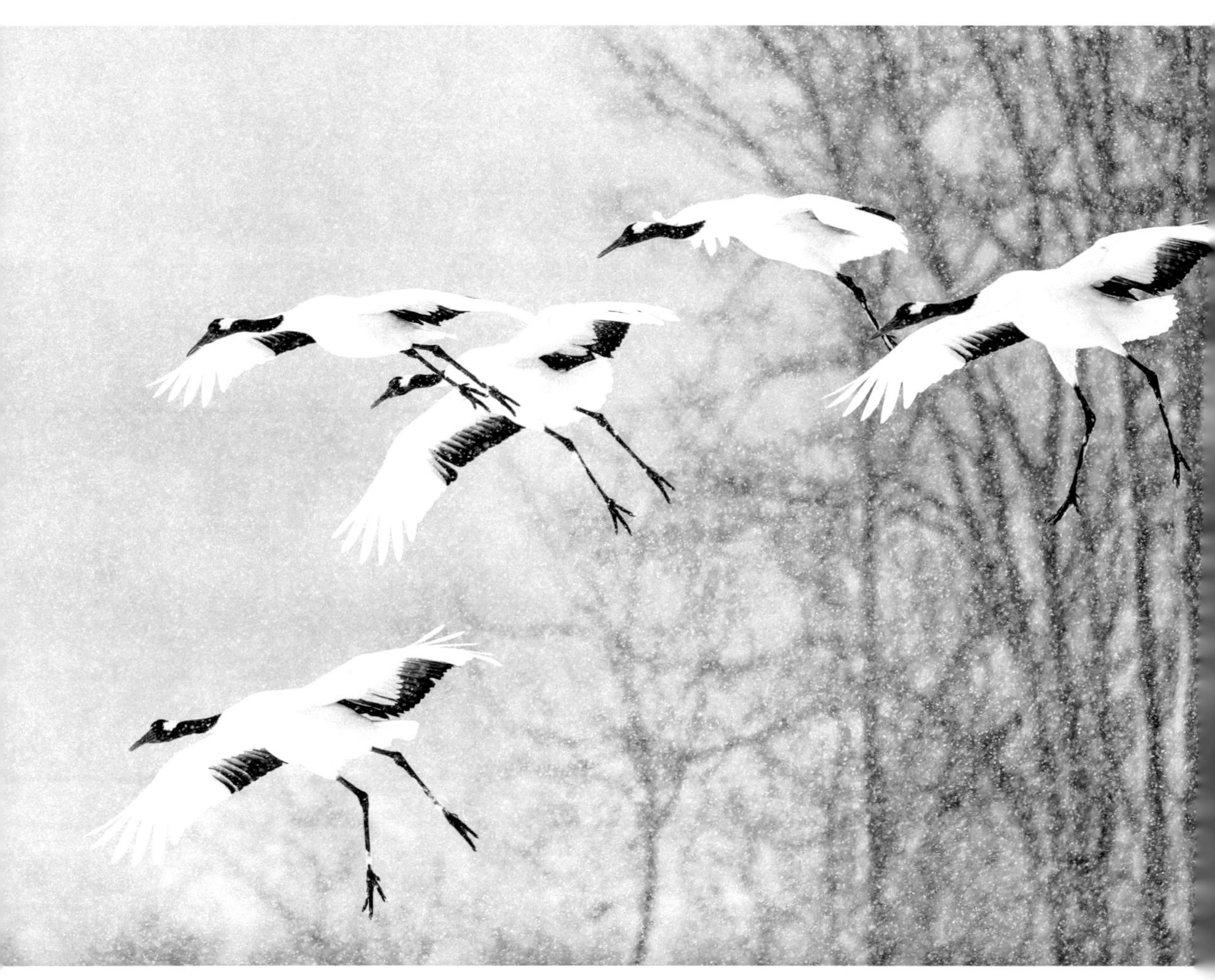

Live today fully, and laugh at the future. Tell yourself:
"The future waits for me—
I am not waiting for the future!"

—Paramahansa Yogananda

Red-crowned Cranes, Hokkaido, Japan Photograph by Markus Varesvuo/Minden Pictures

November/December

29
monday

30
tuesday

1
wednesday

2
thursday

3
friday

NOVEMBER

S	M	T	W	T	F	S
	1	2	3	4	5	6
7	8	9	10	11	12	13
14	15	16	17	18	19	20
21	22	23	24	25	26	27
28	29	30				

4
saturday

DECEMBER

S	M	T	W	T	F	S
			1	2	3	4
5	6	7	8	9	10	11
12	13	14	15	16	17	18
19	20	21	22	23	24	25
26	27	28	29	30	31	

First Quarter ◐

5
sunday

December

6
monday

7
tuesday

8
wednesday

9
thursday

10
friday

11
saturday

12
sunday

DECEMBER

S	M	T	W	T	F	S
			1	2	3	4
5	6	7	8	9	10	11
12	13	14	15	16	17	18
19	20	21	22	23	24	25
26	27	28	29	30	31	

JANUARY 2028

S	M	T	W	T	F	S
						1
2	3	4	5	6	7	8
9	10	11	12	13	14	15
16	17	18	19	20	21	22
23/30	24/31	25	26	27	28	29

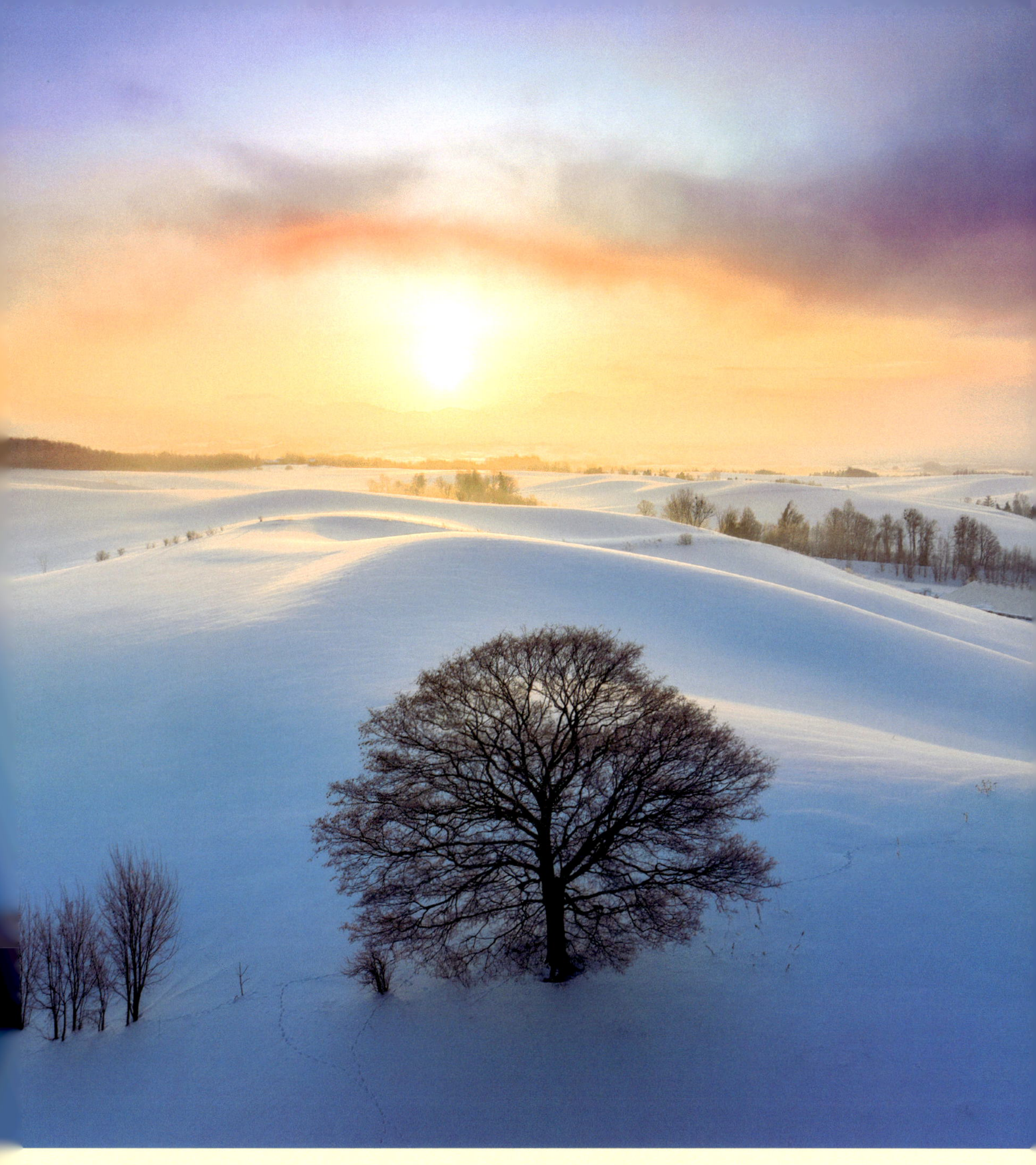

Wait patiently for God's response. He is ever listening to the devotional call of your soul, waiting for you to become fully receptive to His infinite presence.

—Paramahansa Yogananda

Hokkaido, Japan Photograph by Daniel Kordan

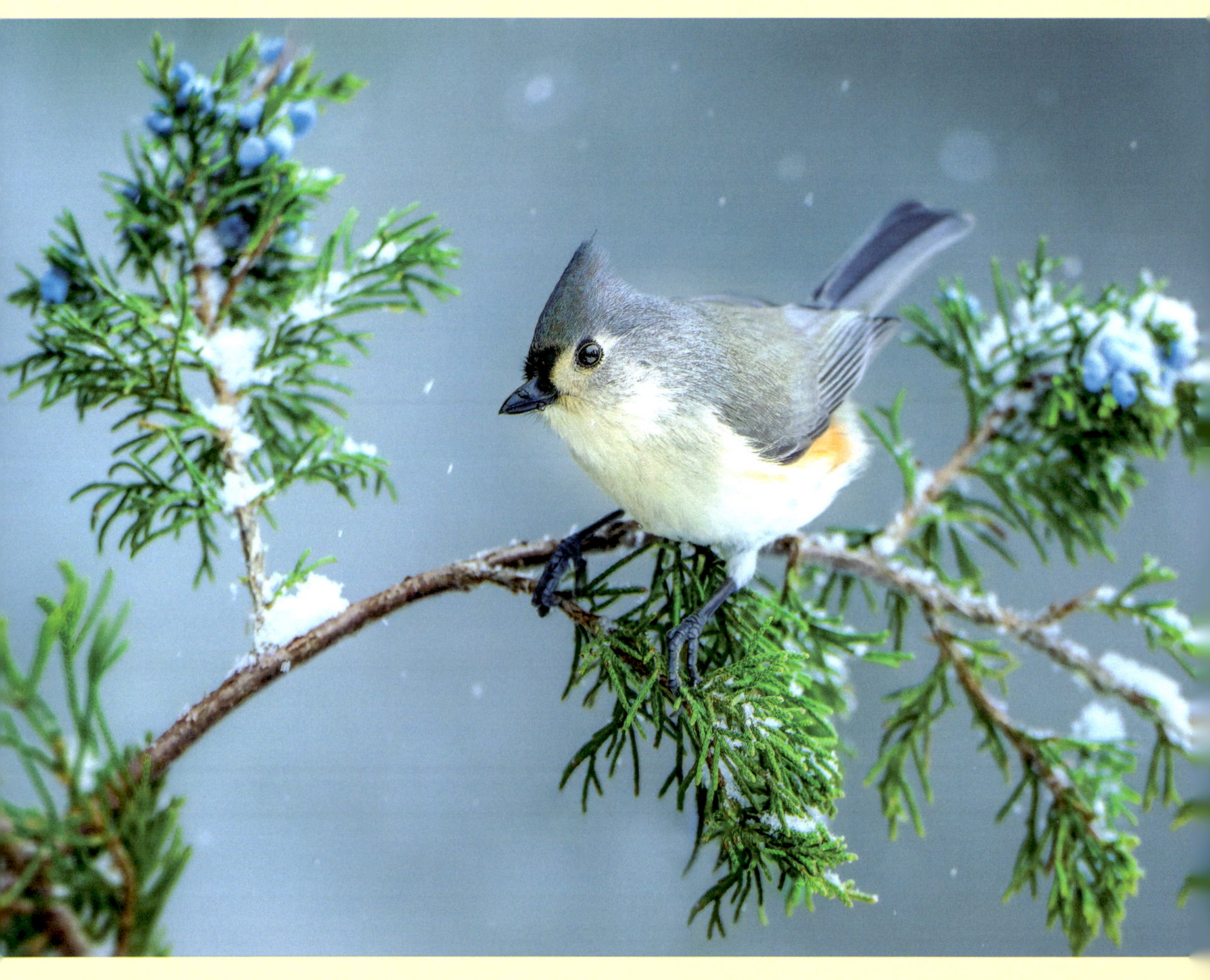

In one sense, God hides Himself; and yet He advertises Himself in the flowers, in the gentle breeze, in the birds, and in all other lovely things.

—Paramahansa Yogananda

Tufted Titmouse, Ontario, Canada   Photograph by Matt Huras/Grandmaison Photography

December

Full Moon ○

13
monday

14
tuesday

15
wednesday

16
thursday

17
friday

DECEMBER

S	M	T	W	T	F	S
			1	2	3	4
5	6	7	8	9	10	11
12	13	14	15	16	17	18
19	20	21	22	23	24	25
26	27	28	29	30	31	

JANUARY 2028

S	M	T	W	T	F	S
						1
2	3	4	5	6	7	8
9	10	11	12	13	14	15
16	17	18	19	20	21	22
23/30	24/31	25	26	27	28	29

18
saturday

19
sunday

December

20
monday

Last Quarter ◑

21
tuesday

UN World Meditation Day   Winter Solstice

22
wednesday

23
thursday

24
friday

Hanukkah begins

25
saturday

Christmas

26
sunday

Boxing Day (Canada, U.K., Australia, N.Z.)

DECEMBER

S	M	T	W	T	F	S
			1	2	3	4
5	6	7	8	9	10	11
12	13	14	15	16	17	18
19	20	21	22	23	24	25
26	27	28	29	30	31	

JANUARY 2028

S	M	T	W	T	F	S
						1
2	3	4	5	6	7	8
9	10	11	12	13	14	15
16	17	18	19	20	21	22
23/30	24/31	25	26	27	28	29

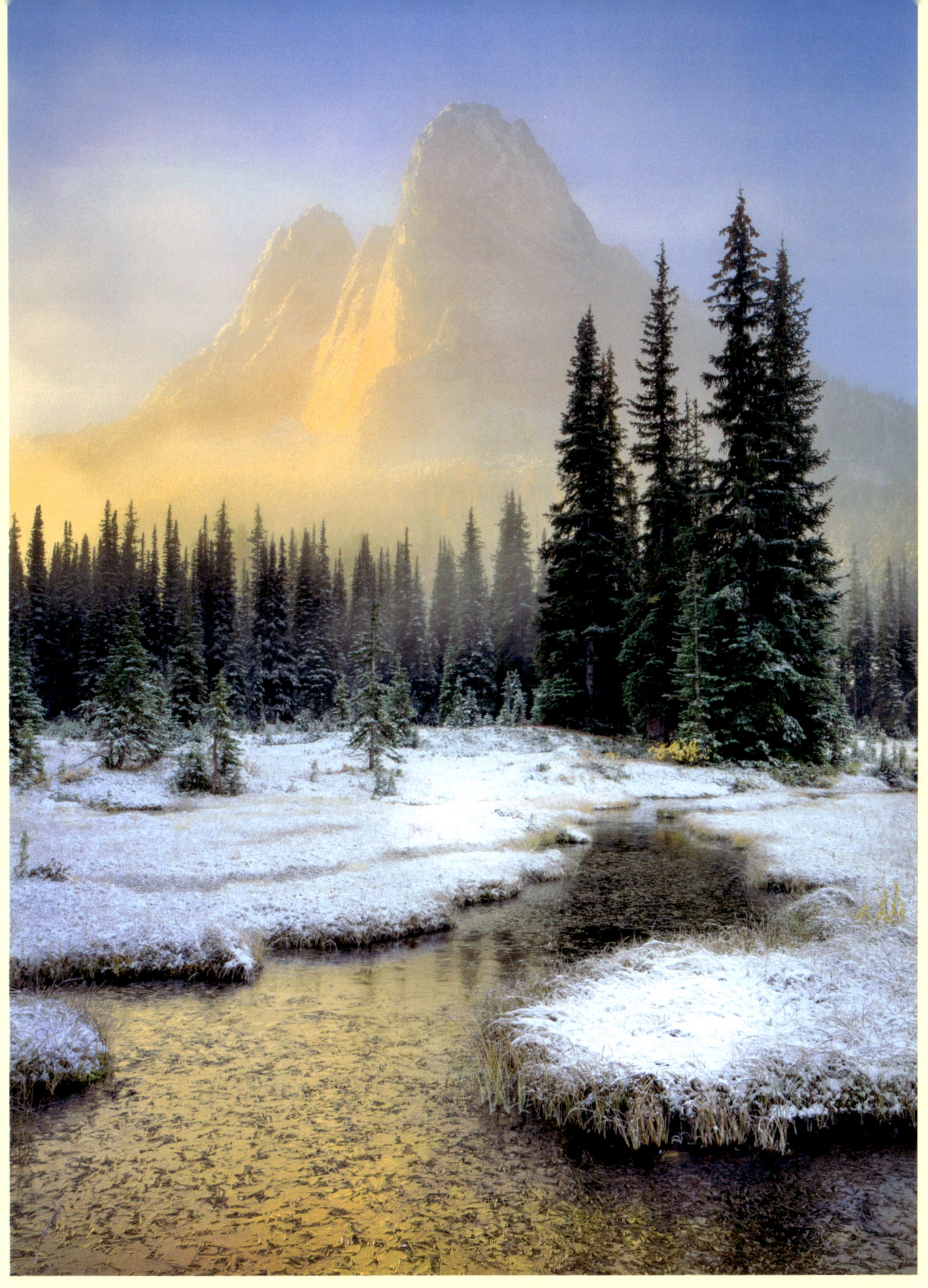

At this time, the angels in the ether celebrate Christmas.
An Infinite Light shone on the earth on that first Christmas day,
and each year at this holy time the ether is filled with that Light.

—Paramahansa Yogananda

Liberty Bell Mountain, North Cascades National Park, Washington   Photograph by Alan Majchrowicz

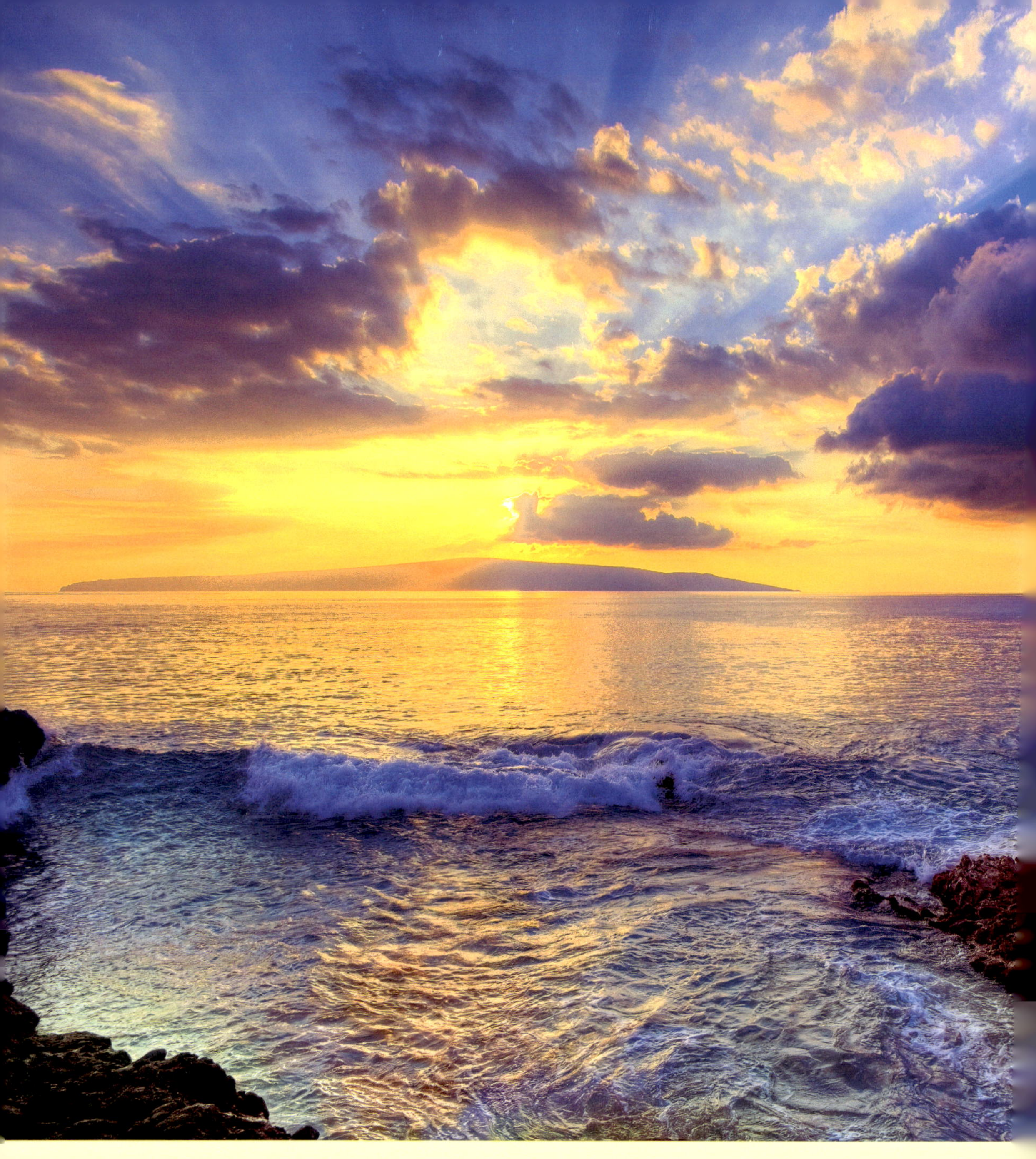

Although you find glimpses of the Divine, don't be satisfied; go deeper within, and you will sit at the brink of eternity facing God.

—Paramahansa Yogananda

Makena, Maui, Hawaii   Photograph by Ron Dahlquist/Image Source

December/January

New Moon ●

27 monday

28 tuesday

29 wednesday

30 thursday

31 friday

New Year's Day

1 saturday

2 sunday

December

S	M	T	W	T	F	S
			1	2	3	4
5	6	7	8	9	10	11
12	13	14	15	16	17	18
19	20	21	22	23	24	25
26	27	28	29	30	31	

January 2028

S	M	T	W	T	F	S
						1
2	3	4	5	6	7	8
9	10	11	12	13	14	15
16	17	18	19	20	21	22
23/30	24/31	25	26	27	28	29

NOTES

ACKNOWLEDGMENTS

We wish to express our sincere appreciation to the following photographers and agencies who contributed to this year's *Inner Reflections* engagement calendar. Following a contributor's name, in parentheses, is the month and day of the week, or other description, where each photo appears.

Bunny Abrams (6/7)

AKM Images (8/16, 8/23)

Robert Barber/AKM Images (8/23)

Gary Bell/Oceanwide Images (2/22)

Espen Bergersen/Minden Pictures (2/1)

Russ Burden (9/13)

David Cobb (3/15)

Ron Dahlquist/Image Source (12/27)

Richard Day (6/28)

Frederick Desmette/Superstock (10/18)

Alan Dyer/AKM Images (8/16)

Guy Edwardes (9/27)

Patrick Endres (1/25)

Tim Fitzharris (3/22, 4/5, 7/5, 7/12, 11/8)

Jeff Foott (1/4)

Dennis Frates (10/11)

Larry Geddis (9/6)

Grandmaison Photography (11/15, 12/13)

Michel Gunther/Superstock (3/29)

John Hendrickson (10/25)

Dean Hueber (2/8, 4/26, 5/24)

Matt Huras/Grandmaison Photography (12/13)

Image Source (12/27)

Mitsuaki Iwago/Superstock (3/1)

Burt Jones & Maurine Shimlock (7/26)

Donald M. Jones/Minden Pictures (1/11)

Daniel Kordan (Front Cover, 2/15, 3/8, 4/19, 5/10, 12/6)

Vadym Lavra (12/28/2026, 6/21, 10/4, 11/22)

Tom & Pat Leeson (7/19)

Lilly/Superstock (4/12)

Vadym Loginov/Superstock (1/18)

Alan Majchrowicz (5/17, 12/20)

Minden Pictures (1/11, 2/1, 8/9, 11/29)

Boyd Norton (6/14, 8/2)

Oceanwide Images (2/22)

Roberta Olenick/Grandmaison Photography (11/15)

Glenn Randall (11/1)

Paul Rezendes (8/30, 9/20)

Scott T. Smith (5/31)

Jim Stamates/Minden Pictures (8/9)

Superstock (1/18, 3/1, 3/29, 4/12, 10/18)

Markus Varesvuo/Minden Pictures (11/29)

Dave Welling (5/3)

About Paramahansa Yogananda

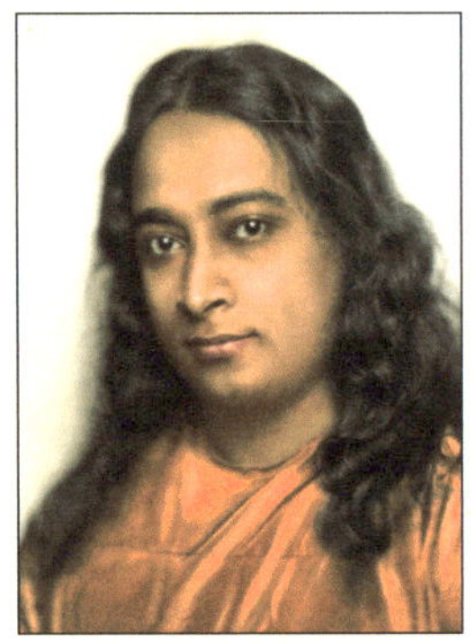

Paramahansa Yogananda
(1893 – 1952)

All the quotes featured in *Inner Reflections* have been selected from the writings of Paramahansa Yogananda, one of the preeminent spiritual teachers of the 20th century. Yogananda came to the United States in 1920 as India's delegate to an international congress of religious leaders convening in Boston. He remained in the West for the better part of the next thirty-two years, conducting classes in cities across America, counseling, and creating a monumental body of written work.

Paramahansa Yogananda's life story, *Autobiography of a Yogi,* is considered a modern spiritual classic. It was selected one of "The Top 100 Spiritual Books of the Twentieth Century" in a survey conducted by HarperCollins. A perennial best seller since it was first published in 1946, *Autobiography of a Yogi* has been translated into more than fifty languages and is widely used in college and university courses.

For more information about SRF publications and the teachings of Paramahansa Yogananda, please visit our website:

www.yogananda.org

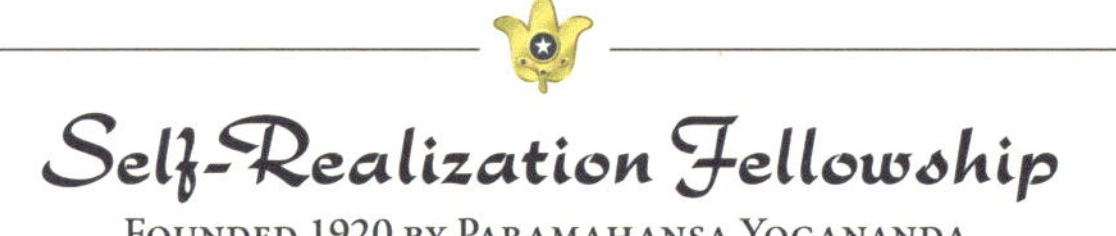

For more than one hundred years Self-Realization Fellowship, the international nonprofit society founded by Paramahansa Yogananda, has been dedicated to carrying on his spiritual and humanitarian work — fostering a spirit of greater harmony and understanding among those of all nations and faiths, and introducing truth-seekers around the world to his universal teachings on the ancient science of yoga.

A SELECTION OF BOOKS BY PARAMAHANSA YOGANANDA

Available at bookstores or from our website:
www.srfbooks.org

Autobiography of a Yogi

Autobiography of a Yogi *(Audiobook, read by Sir Ben Kingsley)*

The Science of Religion

The Law of Success

How You Can Talk With God

Metaphysical Meditations

Scientific Healing Affirmations

The Spiritual Expression of Friendship

Inner Peace: *How to Be Calmly Active and Actively Calm*

Where There Is Light: *Insight and Inspiration for Meeting Life's Challenges*

The Yoga of Jesus: *Understanding the Hidden Teachings of the Gospels*

The Yoga of the Bhagavad Gita: *An Introduction to India's Universal Science of God-Realization*

The Collected Talks and Essays
Volume I: Man's Eternal Quest
Volume II: The Divine Romance
Volume III: Journey to Self-realization
Volume IV: Solving the Mystery of Life

SELF-REALIZATION FELLOWSHIP LESSONS

The scientific techniques of meditation taught by Paramahansa Yogananda, including Kriya Yoga — as well as his guidance on all aspects of balanced spiritual living — are taught in the *Self-Realization Fellowship Lessons*. For more information please visit www.srflessons.org.

SELF-REALIZATION FELLOWSHIP

3880 San Rafael Avenue • Los Angeles, CA 90065-3219

TEL (323) 225-2471 • FAX (323) 225-5088

www.yogananda.org

2026

January

s	m	t	w	t	f	s
				1	2	3
4	5	6	7	8	9	10
11	12	13	14	15	16	17
18	19	20	21	22	23	24
25	26	27	28	29	30	31

February

s	m	t	w	t	f	s
1	2	3	4	5	6	7
8	9	10	11	12	13	14
15	16	17	18	19	20	21
22	23	24	25	26	27	28

March

s	m	t	w	t	f	s
1	2	3	4	5	6	7
8	9	10	11	12	13	14
15	16	17	18	19	20	21
22	23	24	25	26	27	28
29	30	31				

April

s	m	t	w	t	f	s
			1	2	3	4
5	6	7	8	9	10	11
12	13	14	15	16	17	18
19	20	21	22	23	24	25
26	27	28	29	30		

May

s	m	t	w	t	f	s
					1	2
3	4	5	6	7	8	9
10	11	12	13	14	15	16
17	18	19	20	21	22	23
24/31	25	26	27	28	29	30

June

s	m	t	w	t	f	s
	1	2	3	4	5	6
7	8	9	10	11	12	13
14	15	16	17	18	19	20
21	22	23	24	25	26	27
28	29	30				

July

s	m	t	w	t	f	s
			1	2	3	4
5	6	7	8	9	10	11
12	13	14	15	16	17	18
19	20	21	22	23	24	25
26	27	28	29	30	31	

August

s	m	t	w	t	f	s
						1
2	3	4	5	6	7	8
9	10	11	12	13	14	15
16	17	18	19	20	21	22
23/30	24/31	25	26	27	28	29

September

s	m	t	w	t	f	s
		1	2	3	4	5
6	7	8	9	10	11	12
13	14	15	16	17	18	19
20	21	22	23	24	25	26
27	28	29	30			

October

s	m	t	w	t	f	s
				1	2	3
4	5	6	7	8	9	10
11	12	13	14	15	16	17
18	19	20	21	22	23	24
25	26	27	28	29	30	31

November

s	m	t	w	t	f	s
1	2	3	4	5	6	7
8	9	10	11	12	13	14
15	16	17	18	19	20	21
22	23	24	25	26	27	28
29	30					

December

s	m	t	w	t	f	s
		1	2	3	4	5
6	7	8	9	10	11	12
13	14	15	16	17	18	19
20	21	22	23	24	25	26
27	28	29	30	31		

2028

January

s	m	t	w	t	f	s
						1
2	3	4	5	6	7	8
9	10	11	12	13	14	15
16	17	18	19	20	21	22
23/30	24/31	25	26	27	28	29

February

s	m	t	w	t	f	s
		1	2	3	4	5
6	7	8	9	10	11	12
13	14	15	16	17	18	19
20	21	22	23	24	25	26
27	28	29				

March

s	m	t	w	t	f	s
			1	2	3	4
5	6	7	8	9	10	11
12	13	14	15	16	17	18
19	20	21	22	23	24	25
26	27	28	29	30	31	

April

s	m	t	w	t	f	s
						1
2	3	4	5	6	7	8
9	10	11	12	13	14	15
16	17	18	19	20	21	22
23/30	24	25	26	27	28	29

May

s	m	t	w	t	f	s
	1	2	3	4	5	6
7	8	9	10	11	12	13
14	15	16	17	18	19	20
21	22	23	24	25	26	27
28	29	30	31			

June

s	m	t	w	t	f	s
				1	2	3
4	5	6	7	8	9	10
11	12	13	14	15	16	17
18	19	20	21	22	23	24
25	26	27	28	29	30	

July

s	m	t	w	t	f	s
						1
2	3	4	5	6	7	8
9	10	11	12	13	14	15
16	17	18	19	20	21	22
23/30	24/31	25	26	27	28	29

August

s	m	t	w	t	f	s
		1	2	3	4	5
6	7	8	9	10	11	12
13	14	15	16	17	18	19
20	21	22	23	24	25	26
27	28	29	30	31		

September

s	m	t	w	t	f	s
					1	2
3	4	5	6	7	8	9
10	11	12	13	14	15	16
17	18	19	20	21	22	23
24	25	26	27	28	29	30

October

s	m	t	w	t	f	s
1	2	3	4	5	6	7
8	9	10	11	12	13	14
15	16	17	18	19	20	21
22	23	24	25	26	27	28
29	30	31				

November

s	m	t	w	t	f	s
			1	2	3	4
5	6	7	8	9	10	11
12	13	14	15	16	17	18
19	20	21	22	23	24	25
26	27	28	29	30		

December

s	m	t	w	t	f	s
					1	2
3	4	5	6	7	8	9
10	11	12	13	14	15	16
17	18	19	20	21	22	23
24/31	25	26	27	28	29	30

2027

January

s	m	t	w	t	f	s
					1	2
3	4	5	6	7	8	9
10	11	12	13	14	15	16
17	18	19	20	21	22	23
24/31	25	26	27	28	29	30

February

s	m	t	w	t	f	s
	1	2	3	4	5	6
7	8	9	10	11	12	13
14	15	16	17	18	19	20
21	22	23	24	25	26	27
28						

March

s	m	t	w	t	f	s
	1	2	3	4	5	6
7	8	9	10	11	12	13
14	15	16	17	18	19	20
21	22	23	24	25	26	27
28	29	30	31			

April

s	m	t	w	t	f	s
				1	2	3
4	5	6	7	8	9	10
11	12	13	14	15	16	17
18	19	20	21	22	23	24
25	26	27	28	29	30	

May

s	m	t	w	t	f	s
						1
2	3	4	5	6	7	8
9	10	11	12	13	14	15
16	17	18	19	20	21	22
23/30	24/31	25	26	27	28	29

June

s	m	t	w	t	f	s
		1	2	3	4	5
6	7	8	9	10	11	12
13	14	15	16	17	18	19
20	21	22	23	24	25	26
27	28	29	30			

July

s	m	t	w	t	f	s
				1	2	3
4	5	6	7	8	9	10
11	12	13	14	15	16	17
18	19	20	21	22	23	24
25	26	27	28	29	30	31

August

s	m	t	w	t	f	s
1	2	3	4	5	6	7
8	9	10	11	12	13	14
15	16	17	18	19	20	21
22	23	24	25	26	27	28
29	30	31				

September

s	m	t	w	t	f	s
			1	2	3	4
5	6	7	8	9	10	11
12	13	14	15	16	17	18
19	20	21	22	23	24	25
26	27	28	29	30		

October

s	m	t	w	t	f	s
					1	2
3	4	5	6	7	8	9
10	11	12	13	14	15	16
17	18	19	20	21	22	23
24/31	25	26	27	28	29	30

November

s	m	t	w	t	f	s
	1	2	3	4	5	6
7	8	9	10	11	12	13
14	15	16	17	18	19	20
21	22	23	24	25	26	27
28	29	30				

December

s	m	t	w	t	f	s
			1	2	3	4
5	6	7	8	9	10	11
12	13	14	15	16	17	18
19	20	21	22	23	24	25
26	27	28	29	30	31	

January

Sunday	Monday	Tuesday	Wednesday	Thursday	Friday	Saturday
					1	2
3	4	5	6	7	8	9
10	11	12	13	14	15	16
17	18	19	20	21	22	23
24	25	26	27	28	29	30
31						

Jan. 1 New Year's Day
Jan. 5 Paramahansa Yogananda's Birthday
Jan. 18 Martin Luther King, Jr.'s Birthday (Observed)
Jan. 26 Australia Day (Australia)

February

Sunday	Monday	Tuesday	Wednesday	Thursday	Friday	Saturday
	1	2	3	4	5	6
7	8	9	10	11	12	13
14	15	16	17	18	19	20
21	22	23	24	25	26	27
28						

Feb. 14 St. Valentine's Day
Feb. 15 Presidents' Day

March

Sunday	Monday	Tuesday	Wednesday	Thursday	Friday	Saturday
	1	2	3	4	5	6
7	8	9	10	11	12	13
14	15	16	17	18	19	20
21	22	23	24	25	26	27
28	29	30	31			

March 7 Paramahansa Yogananda's Mahasamadhi
March 9 Sri Yukteswar's Mahasamadhi
March 14 Daylight Saving Time begins (U.S. and Canada)
March 17 St. Patrick's Day
March 20 Vernal Equinox
March 26 Good Friday
March 28 Easter Sunday/Daylight Saving Time begins (U.K. and European Union)
March 29 Easter Monday (All except U.S. and Scotland)

April

Sunday	Monday	Tuesday	Wednesday	Thursday	Friday	Saturday
				1	2	3
4	5	6	7	8	9	10
11	12	13	14	15	16	17
18	19	20	21	22	23	24
25	26	27	28	29	30	

April 21 Passover begins

May

Sunday	Monday	Tuesday	Wednesday	Thursday	Friday	Saturday
						1
2	3	4	5	6	7	8
9	10	11	12	13	14	15
16	17	18	19	20	21	22
23	24	25	26	27	28	29
30	31					

May 6 National Day of Prayer
May 9 Mother's Day (U.S., Canada, Australia, N.Z.)
May 10 Sri Yukteswar's Birthday
May 24 Victoria Day (Canada)
May 31 Memorial Day

June

Sunday	Monday	Tuesday	Wednesday	Thursday	Friday	Saturday
		1	2	3	4	5
6	7	8	9	10	11	12
13	14	15	16	17	18	19
20	21	22	23	24	25	26
27	28	29	30			

June 19 Juneteenth
June 20 Father's Day (U.S., Canada, U.K.)
June 21 UN International Day of Yoga
Summer Solstice

July

Sunday	Monday	Tuesday	Wednesday	Thursday	Friday	Saturday
				1	2	3
4	5	6	7	8	9	10
11	12	13	14	15	16	17
18	19	20	21	22	23	24
25	26	27	28	29	30	31

July 1 Canada Day (Canada)
July 4 Independence Day
July 25 Mahavatar Babaji Commemoration Day

August

Sunday	Monday	Tuesday	Wednesday	Thursday	Friday	Saturday
1	2	3	4	5	6	7
8	9	10	11	12	13	14
15	16	17	18	19	20	21
22	23	24	25	26	27	28
29	30	31				

Aug. 25 Janmashtami

September

Sunday	Monday	Tuesday	Wednesday	Thursday	Friday	Saturday
			1	2	3	4
5	6	7	8	9	10	11
12	13	14	15	16	17	18
19	20	21	22	23	24	25
26	27	28	29	30		

Sept. 6 Labor Day (U.S. and Canada)
Sept. 21 UN International Day of Peace
Sept. 22 Autumnal Equinox
Sept. 26 Lahiri Mahasaya's Mahasamadhi
Sept. 30 Lahiri Mahasaya's Birthday

October

Sunday	Monday	Tuesday	Wednesday	Thursday	Friday	Saturday
					1	2
3	4	5	6	7	8	9
10	11	12	13	14	15	16
17	18	19	20	21	22	23
24	25	26	27	28	29	30
31						

Oct. 1 Rosh Hashanah
Oct. 10 Yom Kippur
Oct. 11 Columbus Day/Indigenous Peoples' Day
Thanksgiving Day (Canada)

Oct. 31 Halloween (U.S., Canada, U.K.)
Daylight Saving Time ends
(U.K. and European Union)

NOVEMBER

Sunday	Monday	Tuesday	Wednesday	Thursday	Friday	Saturday
	1	2	3	4	5	6
7	8	9	10	11	12	13
14	15	16	17	18	19	20
21	22	23	24	25	26	27
28	29	30				

Nov. 7 Daylight Saving Time ends (U.S. and Canada)

Nov. 11 Veterans Day
Remembrance Day (Canada)

Nov. 14 Remembrance Sunday (U.K.)

Nov. 25 Thanksgiving Day

December

Sunday	Monday	Tuesday	Wednesday	Thursday	Friday	Saturday
			1	2	3	4
5	6	7	8	9	10	11
12	13	14	15	16	17	18
19	20	21	22	23	24	25
26	27	28	29	30	31	

Dec. 21 UN World Meditation Day
Winter Solstice
Dec. 24 Hanukkah begins
Dec. 25 Christmas
Dec. 26 Boxing Day (Canada, U.K., Australia, N.Z.)

NOTES